A JOURNEY IN PRAYER

WITH MATTHEW HENRY

FOR THE
EDIFICATION OF THE SAINTS
AT
CORNERSTONE CHURCH

BY

AARON STURGILL

CROWDEDSHIP
OUR HOME, AN ANCHOR

Cover art and Book Graphics by Aaron Sturgill
Second edition 2024.

Crowdedship Publications
Waterloo, WI 53594

ISBN 978-1-966583-00-4

To Linda, my wife

Each morning at my side, cups of coffee,
amid our communion with God.
No sweeter moment in the day.

To my kids

I have no greater prayer than,
"May Christ be formed in their souls."

To Mom & Dad

Not only did you model a pursuit in prayer
but have no greater desire than in knowing
your children pursue communion with God.

TABLE OF CONTENTS

ABBREVIATIONS

OT

Amos	Am
1 Chronicles	1 Chr
2 Chronicles	2 Chr
Daniel	Dn
Deuteronomy	Dt
Ecclesiastes	Eccl
Esther	Est
Exodus	Ex
Ezekiel	Eze
Ezra	Ezr
Genesis	Gn
Habakkuk	Hb
Haggai	Hg
Hosea	Hos
Isaiah	Is
Jeremiah	Jer
Job	Jb
Joel	Jl
Jonah	Jon
Joshua	Jo
Judges	Jgs
1 Kings	1 Kgs
2 Kings	2 Kgs
Lamentations	Lam
Leviticus	Lv
Malachi	Mal
Micah	Mi
Nahum	Na
Nehemiah	Neh
Numbers	Num
Obadiah	Ob
Proverbs	Prv
Psalms	Ps
Ruth	Ru
1 Samuel	1 Sm
2 Samuel	2 Sm
Song of Solomon	Sg
Zechariah	Zec
Zephaniah	Zep

NT

Acts	
Colossians	Col
1 Corinthians	1 Cor
2 Corinthians	2 Cor
Ephesians	Eph
Galatians	Gal
Hebrews	Heb
James	Jas
John	Jn
1 John	1 Jn
2 John	2 Jn
3 John	3 Jn
Jude	Jd
Luke	Lk
Mark	Mk
Matthew	Matt
1 Peter	1 Pet
2 Peter	2 Pet
Philippians	Phil
Philemon	Phlm
Revelation	Rv
Romans	Rom
1 Thessalonians	1 Thes
2 Thessalonians	2 Thes
1 Timothy	1 Tim
2 Timothy	2 Tim
Titus	Ti

PREFACE

Background to the journey. My journey in prayer began several years ago from the overflow of two conversations on friendship. Within a month of each other, in the fall of 2015, two church members approached me about what they considered to be a deficit in relationships. As they further described their challenges of belonging and their frustrations for years of church relationships, I took to heart their pain, critique, and desires. In their descriptions, they both acknowledged a desire for friendship. However, a couple questions persisted within my thinking. (1) Is what they want good? Likely, we would agree to the desire for friendship being generally healthy and appropriate. Nagging speculations concerning motivation and responsibility from this question eventually subsided. However, the second question pricked my mind for years. (2) Is the church responsible to help facilitate friendships? And, more personally, am I, as the pastor, responsible for facilitating the friendships of church members? More broadly speaking, what types of relationships should the church facilitate?

I had recently started a doctoral program in biblical counseling at The Southern Baptist Theological Seminary, and for my project, decided to pursue a deeper understanding of friendship and its role in church life. Sickness in our home would prolong this journey, lead to a ThM at Southern in December of 2017, and sideline my formal study on friendship. In God's providence and by his good grace, I began my doctorate once again in the Fall of 2018, this time at Southeastern Baptist Theological Seminary. The head of my program quickly transitioned my project from friendship to biblical fellowship. While initially irritating, I would come to realize an understanding of biblical fellowship answered my questions concerning relationships within the church.

How do we get to prayer? As part of my project, I formed a fellowship team consisting of nearly a dozen of my church members. While much of our month-long discussion surrounded an understanding of biblical fellowship, our final task consisted of formulating a proposal to enhance biblical fellowship at Cornerstone Church. The team determined one of our church's greatest weaknesses in biblical fellowship to be a lack of prayer in both our personal lives and our church life. For Cornerstone to enhance its biblical fellowship, we would need to pursue a better understanding and practice of prayer. The fellowship team proposed we focus on four themes over the next four years – prayer, discipleship, the Holy Spirit, and communion. So then, in the Fall of 2021, I began gathering resources for a study on prayer.

Throughout the next year, I would be introduced to authors ranging from the 17th century Reverend Thomas Ken and Martin Luther to the 19th century Samuel Miller to helpful authors in the 20th and 21st centuries such as Donald Whitney, Leonard Ravenhill, Scotty Smith, Megan Hill, Ole Hallesby, and Walter Brueggemann. While searching for helpful resources, I quickly noticed several authors referencing one particular resource – Matthew Henry's *A Method for Prayer*.

Throughout the following months, I found myself consistently, if not daily, going back to Henry's book to be refreshed by his approach to prayer. However, I found his archaic language challenging and started rewording his paragraphs. At first, I felt disrespectful in changing any of his thoughts and wording. But quickly, I came to embrace the value of personalizing each prayer. Early each morning, in the dim light of my den even further darkened by the comforting terracotta orange walls, as part of my communion with God, I would take a single paragraph, meditate on its verses, and rewrite the paragraph as a personal prayer. Often one paragraph would bleed into a couple days if not a week, causing the journey through Henry's book to last several years.

Amid this journey, I came to further appreciate the statement, "the joy is in the journey."

My Motivation. Throughout this journey, primarily, four people groups compelled my forward progress. First, I need to grow in prayer. Throughout my personal journey with the Lord, I have consistently prayed. However, my prayer life mostly reflected a quote from the 19th century, Pentecostal evangelist, Smith Wigglesworth. He once said, "I don't often spend more than half an hour in prayer at one time, but I never go more than half an hour without praying."[1] While this statement may have reflected my prayer life at times, sadly the phrase also seemed to justify a lack of lengthy times of prayer. My most recent journey in prayer dismisses the first half of the statement while

---

[1] For years, I thought this statement derived from a different source. I can't find an original source for this quote, but consistently those who quote this statement attribute the phrase to Smith Wigglesworth.

attempting to retain the second half. My time of morning prayer[2] now often takes up to two hours, if not more. However, I still desire to go very little time without praying.

Second, my wife has accompanied me throughout this journey. For years, Linda and I desired to have a consistent devotional and prayer time together. While consistently maintaining personal devotions, we struggled finding the right time to pray and read together. When she rose early for her morning devotional time, I would momentarily lay in bed, shame ridden, desiring to get up with her. However, typically, I successfully rid myself of the shame and rolled back over to sleep. In contrast, my mind would find its clearest moments late in the evening as my dear wife struggled to stay awake. Over more than twenty years of marriage, we attempted to find some consistent devotional time together with very little success. God, in his grace, used two challenging moments to assist in this pursuit. First, Covid forced us to stay home. We contend, Covid gifted us a consistent devotional and prayer time. The change in schedule allowed us to spend time together just a little later in the morning when my mind was more alert. Second, God used a year and a half of insomnia, coupled with a particular medication, to reprogram my sleep patterns. Previously, I struggled to get up before 7:00. However, these two catalysts shifted my morning routine up by about two hours. Coupled together, Covid and insomnia led to an early morning devotional time for Linda and

---

[2] I have chosen to not make clear distinctions between prayer, devotions, scripture reading, or Bible study. In overly simplified fashion, I consider prayer as my communication to God and scripture reading (or Bible study) as God's communication to me. Combined, they form my *communion* with God. Therefore strictly speaking, my prayer serves as one component of my entire time. Some days prayer takes up most of the time, whereas on other days, reading and study consume more time.

me – now my favorite time of day. My journey with Matthew Henry became a significant part of these moments.

Third, I can think of no greater, tangible gift to my children than a resource for their enhanced prayer life. Sadly, for years, the consistency in my prayers for my children reflected the same inconsistency in my overall prayer life. Developing a consistent and substantive prayer time resulted in purposeful and daily intercession for my children. Linda and I have often joked, "if you were on a deserted island and could only pray one thing, what would it be?" We agree we would pray one specific line from Matthew Henry's prayer for our children, "we earnestly pray that Christ may be formed in their souls."[3] We couldn't think of any eternal, substantive request that did not somehow fit within that one request.

Finally, I desired to finish this resource for the equipping of my church family for greater prayer. All along, the edification of Cornerstone Church served as the initial impetus for studying prayer. While God gifted me so many other blessings through this journey, I always wanted to personally grow in my understanding and practice of prayer in order to benefit my church family. As I read Henry's book, I would often struggle with archaic words and at times challenging sentence structure. I often spent as much time interpreting Henry as I did resonating with his point in my own prayer. I wanted my church to have a similar resource as Henry's book but in a format that would be more accessible to them.

---

[3] Matthew Henry, "A Prayer Proper to be Put Up By Parents for Their Children," in *A Method for Prayer*, 263.

INTRODUCTION

Approach to this edition. Isaac Watts summarized Henry's approach in organizing his prayer points and scripture passages. Watts wrote,

> Mr. Henry's method of prayer is a judicious collection of scriptures, proper to the several parts of that duty.... And above all, I would recommend to them the late Mr. Henry's Method of Prayer, where the devout expressions of the holy men of God, in scripture, are ranged under a variety of heads or common places, suited to the several parts of prayer, and the different occasions of the Christian life.

Henry offers a thorough organization of prayer topics accompanied by a helpful list of verses pertinent to the topic. While often Henry took some liberty in combining verses into one sentence or adding a prefatory statement, he primarily just listed verses, often with conceptual redundancies throughout the verse list. In other words, he doesn't offer a prayer but the resources for prayer.

On the other hand, I attempted to take the verse list and formulate a single prayer, which often required combining of verses, deletion of redundancies, change of tense, and the change of verses discussing God to a prayer directed to God.

In some sense, I offer nothing new. Others, well suited to the task, have come before me offering a modernized version of Henry's work. O. Palmer Robertson offers a very helpful resource, titled *A Way to Pray* by Matthew Henry. Robertson retains Henry as author and offers this resource as a modernized edition of Henry's book.

Robertson does simplify Henry's excessive outline structure of each chapter, which extends, at times, to five layers of outlining. While Robertson offers a different version for the scripture passages, he appears to retain all of Henry's passages.[4] In contrast, I often deleted or added other scripture passages to a particular prayer point. Robertson describes his edition in the following manner.

> This current edition does not represent simply an effort to modernize the language of Matthew Henry's original. Instead, it is an effort to provide a respectful but thorough reworking of the text of Matthew Henry in light of careful exegetical consideration … The reader of this revised edition will find that it falls more in the category of 'dynamic' rather than 'literal' renderings of scripture. This approach is justified in large part by the fact that the effort is being made to make the reading as natural as possible in the language of today so that the reader will be able to express himself naturally before God in his mother tongue (xv).

Ligon Duncan also offers a very helpful edition of Henry's work. Through the Alliance of Confessing Evangelicals, Duncan offers both a physical copy and online copy of the resource. The online copy offers several translations (ESV, KJV, NAS, and NIV) for each passage as

---

[4] I assume Robertson primarily keeps all of Henry's verse choices because in all the prayers I compared they were the same. I did not check each paragraph with the intention of checking Robertson's verse decisions, so he may have possibly changed, deleted, or added some passages. In his introduction, Robertson does admit to adding a few prayers to the book (i.e. a prayer for baptized adults). Robertson writes, "At some points, new or additional material has been introduced where it seemed useful or appropriate" (xiv). His changes appear to be more in the organization of chapters and the rewording of verses rather than in verse selection.

well as a first person and corporate reading of each version. Unlike Robertson, Duncan does not offer his own translation work but instead employs four of the most popular English translations. Duncan does not change any of Henry's verse selections.

I am extremely thankful for the work of these two men and their accompanying teams, for they offer a wonderful gift to the church and to me personally. Their work has often accompanied my journey with Matthew Henry in prayer. In my writing, I do not attempt to offer something better, but rather the byproduct of my own personal prayer life. As a result, my writing would not equate to an edition of Henry's work. While I always started with his verse list for each prayer point, I regularly deleted, added, and compressed scripture passages. I also attempted to make each prayer point into one cohesive prayer rather than a list of verses. Often, the text reflects the point of a verse and not the wording.

Out of deep respect for Henry, I originally structured the book as closely as possible to Henry's outline.[5] The most significant exception to this structure was my deletion of several of Henry's intercessory prayers in chapter five. Having finished my original edition, I then decided to reorganize the prayers to offer a clearer resource with less outlining.

---

[5] There are several editions for Henry's work, not including Robertson's and Duncan's. In looking at different editions, I often found disparity in some of the outlining. Therefore, I chose one edition as the primary reference for my outlining. The publisher offers no date other than the date at the end of Henry's introduction, March 25, 1710. The Internet Archive dates the book as 1714. All my original outlining, save those few exceptions, adheres to the structure of this version. The version may be found and downloaded at the following website. https://archive.org/details/methodforprayerw0000henr

Additional assessment of Henry's work. Matthew Henry reflects impeccable biblical logic. In my devotions, I would often sit pondering on his particular wording or passage selection – usually to realize a helpful word choice or an unexpected passage. Truly, this process was a delight. However, I was often surprised at his lack of New Testament (NT) use. His prayer points seemed excessive in Old Testament (OT) passages, even when NT texts seemed obvious. Clearly, Henry views the connection between Israel and the Church differently than I do which likely explains much of the confusion.

I'm uncertain as to my level of theological disagreement with Henry. Besides his view of Israel and the Church, a couple other differences presented themselves, for instance his inclusion of a prayer for infant baptism. I assumed some theological differences by his use of particular passages, even though I'm uncertain as to what he may have been thinking. On these occasions, when I sensed Henry missed the author's original point, I simply deleted those verses and often replaced them with passages I thought more clear to the point.

Henry consistently offers hope or appropriate conclusions throughout his writing, but typically this hope came by following the logic of the whole book rather than offering hope in each section or paragraph. I often chose to place a little hope at the end of each paragraph – especially in the chapter on confession.

I deleted several prayers in chapter five concerning national unity, morality, etc. In these cases, Henry applied passages to a modern nation that were specifically intended for Israel. The practical elements of those prayers could be found in other prayers – for instance praying for the gospel to spread, praying for revival in a nation, or praying for unity within the church.

My approach to Henry's work. *Chapter choice and structure.* Henry's work included four additional chapters (6-9). While I personally found these chapters helpful, I chose not to include them. Henry's first five chapters consisted of scripture passages. However, by means of his last four, he offered a host of prayers for specific occasions, not connected to specific passages. I found a few of these prayers to be extremely helpful, but on the whole, I determined both myself and my intended audience would find much less help in that format.

In this edition, I almost entirely ignored Henry's outline. Henry only used numbers (not numbers and letters) even though he had several layers of sub points. When Henry got to the fifth sublevel, the outline became challenging to follow. While keeping the five major chapter headings, and the general order of prayers, I reorganized the prayers and avoided the traditional outlining (i.e. I.A.1.a.) for what I consider to be a clearer organization. To do so, I added some headings and truncated sub-points.

Scripture wording and versions used. Each morning, I typically opened Henry's book, my Word document, and my bible program with about 10 different versions. I would read all the passages, meditating on meaning, Henry's logic, and how the list of verses might form a single, cohesive prayer. As time went on, I most frequently used the ESV, NLT, or NET while also often employing the wording from the NIV or HCSB. In my prayers, I do not offer a translation of any of these verses, but instead desired to meditate on the verses and offer a timeless, if not timely interpretation to its intent.

Sentence Perspective. Most of Henry's statements consisted of a direction as to what we ought to do. I changed this throughout to statements of what we are doing. For example, Henry writes, "we must solemnly address ourselves to that infinitely great and glorious being," which I changed to, "we praise the infinite and glorious being." (2) Additionally, Henry kept the tense of the verse. Often the verse referred to God or was a statement by God. In each of these instances, I changed the prayer to be a direct address to God rather than about him. (3) I attempted to write the way I would speak so that these prayers could serve as personal and corporate prayers. (4) I was inconsistent with my use of the plural and singular. Some prayers seemed overly personal, and I would use single person. Whereas others seemed more corporate, and I would employ the plural person. These decisions likely came as a result of that particular day's circumstances rather than some objective criteria. (5) I did choose to use contractions – probably not consistently throughout – so that the prayers were more conversational.

1.

ADORATION OF GOD

The steadfast love of the Lord never ceases, and his mercies never come to an end. They are new every morning. Great is your faithfulness (Lam 3:21-22). Therefore, let us lift up our hearts and hands to heaven (Lam 3:41). You desire we come and talk with you. My heart has heard and responds with, Lord I am coming (Ps 27:8). We honor you for the glory due your name. We worship you in the splendor of your holiness (Ps 29:2). We give our lives to you (Ps 25:1). So then, with boldness, we enter heaven's Most Holy Place because the blood of Jesus opened a new and life-giving way (Heb 10:19–20). Therefore, we strive to come without distraction (1 Cor 7:35), honoring you with our lips and drawing near with our hearts (Matt 15:8); for you are looking for those who will worship you in spirit and in truth (Jn 4:23-24).

1.1. The great and glorious God.

We praise the infinitely great and glorious God, possessing full belief in his presence and a holy awe and reverence for his majesty. We address God with expressions such as the following: Holy, holy, holy, is the Lord God Almighty, who was and is and is to come! (Rv 4:8). You alone we call Lord. You are the Most High over all the earth (Ps 83:18). O God, you are our God; we seek you earnestly; our souls thirst for you (Ps 63:1). You are our strength and song and have become our salvation. We praise you and exalt you (Ex 15:2). You are the one, true, and living God and everlasting King (Jer 10:10; 1 Thes 1:9; Dt 6:4).

We distinguish between ourselves and those who worship false gods. Their idols are silver and gold, the work of human hands (Ps 115:4). Those who make them and trust in them become like them (Ps 115:8). Those idols are worthless, a work of delusion. But the God of Israel is no idol! He is the Creator of everything that exists. The Lord of hosts is his name (Jer 10:15-16). He is God who rules over everything and is worthy of eternal praise (Rom 9:5). Their rock is not like our Rock (Dt 32:31). Their gods who did not make the heavens and earth will vanish from the earth and from under the heavens (Jer 10:11). However, Lord, you are our eternal Rock who endures forever, and your fame is known to every generation (Ps 135:13).

1.2. God as transcendently bright.

We reverently adore God and give him glory for he is transcendently bright and holy, self-existent and self-sufficient, an infinite and eternal Spirit, that has all perfections in Himself. Lord, you are my God and with all that I am, I praise you because of your greatness! You are clothed with splendor and majesty, covering yourself with light as with a garment (Ps 104:1-2). But, to us, you have covered yourself in darkness, like a canopy of dark storm clouds around you (Ps 18:11). So, teach us how to speak to you, for we do not know how to approach you because of the darkness (Jb 37:19). This is the message you have declared; you are light and in you is no darkness at all (1 Jn 1:5). You are also love, and everyone who resides in love resides in you, and you reside in them (1 Jn 4:16). While we stumble and struggle due to the darkness, you are the Father of lights who does not change like shifting shadows. Every generous act and perfect gift come down to us from you (Jas 1:17). You are the blessed and only Sovereign, King of kings and Lord of lords, who alone possesses immortality and lives in such brilliant light that no human has ever seen or is able to see you. All honor and power are yours forever (1 Tim 6:16).

We embrace God's existence as unquestionable. Lord, the heavens declare your glory, and the skies above proclaim the work of your hands (Ps 19:1). Since your creation of the world and through all that you have made, you have displayed your invisible qualities, especially your eternal power and divine nature; so much so that all people are without excuse. Yet, foolish man, darkened in his mind, did not honor you or give you thanks (Rom 1:20-21). Only fools say in their hearts, "There is no God" (Ps 14:1). Therefore, we come to you in faith, believing you exist and reward those who seek you (Heb 11:6).

Yet, we also acknowledge God's nature as incomprehensible. While Job's friends offered poor counsel, Zophar correctly reminded Job, "we cannot fathom your mysteries or your depths; we cannot discover the limits of your perfections" (Jb 11:7). We are incapable of fully recounting all your mighty acts or relating all your praiseworthy deeds (Ps 106:2). Even though no one can fathom your greatness, you remain unquestionably great and worthy of our praise (Ps 145:3).

And his perfections to be matchless and without comparison. Lord, among the gods, no others exist like you. Unlike any other, you are majestic in holiness, awesome in glorious deeds, performing wonders (Ex 15:11, Ps 86:8). No created thing possesses your power nor can thunder with a voice like yours (Jb 40:9). No one in all of heaven compares to you; not even the mightiest angel is anything like you, Lord. The great angelic assembly stands in awe of you. You are far more awesome than all those who surround your throne (Ps 89:6-7).

All the nations you created will one day bow before you and honor your name because of your greatness and marvelous deeds. You alone are God (Ps 86:9-10).

And that God is infinitely above us and all other beings. While our actions are typically driven by our emotions, Lord, you are not a man (Hos 11:9). You do not have eyes like us or see or perceive things like humans. Your days are not short like ours or your years like the years of man (Jb 10:4-5). Rather, as the heavens are higher than the earth, your ways are higher than our ways and your thoughts higher than our thoughts (Is 55:9). Entire nations are but a drop in the bucket compared to you. They are nothing more than dust on the scale. All the nations of the world are worth nothing to you. You count them less than nothing and mere emptiness (Is 40:15-17).

1.2.1. God is eternally unchanging.

God, you are the eternal King, immortal and invisible, deserving and receiving all honor and glory forever and ever. You alone are God (1 Tim 1:17). Even before the mountains were born, you brought the world into being. From beginning to end you are God (Ps 90:2). As the radiance of your glory, Jesus Christ is as well the same yesterday and today and forever (Heb 1:3, 13:8). Long ago you laid the foundation of the earth, and the heavens are the work of your hands. They will perish, but you will remain; they will all wear out like a garment. You will change them like a robe, and they will pass away, but you are the same, and your years have no end (Ps 102:25–27). You do not faint or grow weary, and your understanding is unsearchable (Is 40:28). Because you do not change, we are not consumed (Mal 3:6).

1.2.2. God is present everywhere.

Through the prophet Jeremiah, to those who thought they could either hide from you or avoid your wrath, you asked the question, "Am I only a God nearby, and not a God far off?" No one can hide themselves where you cannot see them. You fill all the heavens and the earth (Jer 23:23-24). Even though you have spread all mankind throughout the earth and sovereignly appointed each one of us boundaries and moments of time from which we seek and hope to find you, you are not far from any one of us (Acts 17:26-27). I can never escape from your Spirit! I can never get away from your presence! If I go up to heaven, you are there; if I go down to the grave, you are there. If I ride the wings of the morning, if I dwell by the farthest oceans, even there your hand will guide me, and your strength will support me. I could ask the darkness to hide me and the light around me to become night— but even in darkness I cannot hide from you. To you the night shines as bright as day. Darkness and light are the same to you (Ps 139:7-12).

1.2.3. God perfectly knows and seesall.

Lord, nothing in all creation is hidden from you. Before your eyes, everything is naked and exposed, and we are accountable to you (Heb 4:13). Your eyes search the whole earth, keeping an eye on the evil and the good (Prv 15:3), and strengthening those who are devoted to you (2 Chr 16:9). You search hearts and test minds in order to give to everyone what their actions deserve (Jer 17:10). You have searched me and known me. You know when I sit and when I stand. You understand my thoughts from far away. You observe my travels and my rest; You are aware of all my ways. Before a word is on my tongue,

You know all about it. This extraordinary knowledge is beyond me. It is lofty; I am unable to reach it (Ps 139:1-4, 6).

1.2.4. God's wisdom is unsearchable.

Lord, your understanding possesses no limits. Not only have you created and counted every star but have also called each one by name (Ps 147:4-5). Your providential care of your creation reveals your counsel as wonderful and your wisdom as excellent (Is 28:29). Your wisdom is profound and your power vast (Jb 9:4). Lord, your works are countless. In wisdom you have made them all. The earth is full of your creatures (Ps 104:24), having worked out everything in conformity to the counsel of your will (Eph 1:11). Oh, the immeasurable depth of your riches, wisdom, and knowledge. It is impossible for me to understand your decisions and ways (Rom 11:33).

1.2.5. God's sovereignty is indisputable.

Lord, the heavens are Your heavens (Ps 115:16a), and the earth is Yours and the fullness thereof, the world and those who dwell therein (Ps 24:1). In Your hand are the depths of the earth; the heights of the mountains are also Yours. The sea is yours, for you made it, and your hands formed the dry land (Ps 95:4-5). Every beast of the forest is yours, and all that moves in the field is yours (Ps 50:10-11). Therefore, Lord, you are a great God, and a great King above all gods (Ps 95:3).

1.2.6. God's power is irresistible.

Man cannot control or manipulate God's power yet can accomplish nothing without it.

God, all power belongs to you (Ps 62:11). Nothing is impossible for you (Lk 1:37). You can do everything, and no one can prevent you from accomplishing your purpose (Jb 42:2). There is no other god like you. You are the one who kills and gives life; you are the one who wounds and heals; no one can be rescued from your powerful hand! (Dt 32:39). Like Abraham, I give you glory, being convinced you are able to perform all that you have promised (Rom 4:19-21). And gloriously, you gave all power in heaven and earth to Jesus Christ, so we go, with certainty, proclaiming your gospel to all nations (Matt 28:18).

1.2.7. God is perfectly pure and morally right.

Lord, You are the Rock; your deeds are perfect. Everything you do is just and fair. You are a faithful God who does no wrong (Dt 32:4). We declare, you are our rock. There is no evil in you (Ps 92:15). You are righteous and filled with kindness in everything you do (Ps 145:17). Therefore, your rules are completely reliable and holiness adorns your house for endless days (Ps 93:5).

1.2.8. God is just in the oversight of His creation.

Lord, you have always been righteous and just when I complain to you (Jer 12:1). It is impossible for you to do wrong, and as the Almighty to act unjustly. You repay a person according to his deeds (Jb 34:10-11). Therefore, You are also always just when you confront me, and right when you condemn me (Ps 51:4). Your righteousness is like the highest mountains; Your judgments, like the deepest sea (Ps 36:6). Even though you are veiled in mystery, righteousness and justice are the foundation of your throne (Ps 97:2).

1.2.9. God's truths are absolute and the treasures of His goodness unlimited.

Lord, I thank you, for you are good, and your faithful love endures forever (Ps 136:1, 117:2, 100:5). You are a compassionate God and slow to anger. You lavish unfailing love to a thousand generations, forgiving iniquity, rebellion, and sin (Ex 34:6-7). This is why we run to you and are safe, for you are our strong tower (Prv 18:10). Truly, you are good to everyone and shower your compassion on all your creation (Ps 145:9, 119:68). Reveal yourself to us (Ex 33:19). Keep your loving kindness before our eyes (Ps 26:3) that we may taste and see that you are good. What joy we experience as we take refuge in you (Ps 34:8).

1.2.10. God's glorious attributes extend far beyond man's most exhaustive descriptions of God's divine nature.

Job saw a magnificent display of your power and still declared, "these are but the outer fringe of your ways, and how small a whisper we hear of you. Who then can comprehend the thunder of your power?" (Jb 26:14). You are beyond our reach and exalted in power (Jb 37:23). Like the Levites, I stand and praise you, my God, who lives from everlasting to everlasting. May your glorious name be praised! May it be exalted above all blessing and praise! (Neh 9:5).

1.3. God's heavenly glory.

We acknowledge and praise God for the splendor of his heavenly glory. You have made the heavens your throne; from there you rule over everything (Ps 103:19), from a throne, high and lifted up, attended by mighty seraphim (Is 6:1-2). In your grace towards us, you obscure the view of your heavenly throne by spreading clouds over it (Jb 26:9). From your throne, you send your ministering angels like the wind and flames of fire, to serve your people (Ps 104:4; Heb 1:7;14). Daniel describes your future judgment where a river of fire flows from your throne, while thousands upon thousands serve you and ten thousand times ten thousand stand before you (Dn 7:9). All those in your presence carry out your plans, obey your orders, and do your will (Ps 103:20-21). And, in faith, we come to Mount Zion, the city of the living God, and to an assembly of myriads of angels, and to the church of the firstborn, and to you, the God and judge of all, and to Jesus our Mediator (Heb 12:22-24).

1.4. God as Creator, Sustainer, and Sovereign.

We praise God as the Creator, Sustainer, and Sovereign over all his creation. Lord, you are worthy to receive glory and honor and power because you have created all things, and because of your will they exist and were created (Rv 4:11, 14:7). We fear and stand in awe for you spoke and it came into existence; you commanded and it stood fast (Ps 33:9, Gn 1). And, your creation stands firm to this day because all things are your servants (Ps 119:90-91). The day is yours, also the night; you established the moon and the sun. You set all the boundaries of the earth; you made summer and winter (Ps 74:16-17). You uphold all things by the word of your power (Heb 1:3), and in you all things hold together (Col 1:17). Your creation, full of your creatures, reveals your wisdom (Ps 104:23-24), righteousness, and justice (Ps 36:6). They all look to you to provide their food at the proper time. Your hand satisfies the desire of every living thing (Ps 145:15-16, 36:6); not even a sparrow falls to the ground without your consent (Matt 10:29). You alone are the Lord. You have made heaven, the heaven of heavens, with all their host, the earth and all that is on it, the seas and all that is in them; and you preserve all of them; and the host of heaven worships you (Neh 9:6, Ps 103:19).

And, you made man from the dust of the ground and breathed into his nostrils the breath of life, and he became a living being (Gn 2:7), for which you have determined his appointed times and boundaries (Acts 17:26). Thankfully, you rule the kingdom of men and give it to whom you choose (Dn 4:25). While we typically desire the favor of our rulers, it is from you that one gets justice (Prv 29:26).

Hallelujah! For the Lord our God the Almighty reigns (Rv 19:6) and accomplishes all things according to his plan (Eph 1:11).

1.5. God's Triunity.

We honor, with distinction, the three persons of the godhead, Father, Son, and Holy Spirit, each possessing distinct roles in creation and redemption, while only one God. God, I praise you as being one God (Dt 6:4-5; 1 Kgs 8:60; Is 45:5-6) in three distinct persons (Matt 3:16-17, 28:19; 1 Cor 12:4-6, 2 Cor 13:14; Phil 2:1).

I thank you, Father, Lord of heaven and earth (Matt 11:25) for, in the beginning, you created all things, and because of your will they exist and were created (Rv 4:11, 14:7, Gn 1:1), yet you graciously revealed yourself to simple people like us, bringing us rest through your Son (Matt 11:25-29). In the beginning, the Son already existed, was with God, and was God. The Son, who gave life to everything and brought light to everyone, became flesh, dwelt among us, and revealed your glory (Jn 1:1-4, 14). You desire everyone to honor the Son just as they honor you (Jn 5:23), so we join the angels in praising the Son because he is the radiance of your glory and the exact imprint of your nature (Heb 1:6, 3).

I praise you, Son, for you are the faithful witness, the firstborn from the dead, and the ruler of the kings of earth (Rv 1:5), acknowledging the lofty position in which the Father placed you, bowing my knee to your authority, and confessing you are Lord, to the glory of God the Father (Phil 2:9-11).

I praise you, Holy Spirit and Helper, sent by the Son from the Father, in order to testify of the Son (Jn 15:26) and teach us all things (Jn 14:26). Gloriously, you carried along the men who would proclaim God's revelation to his people (2 Pe 1:21). Thank you for your conviction (Jn 16:8-9), eternal sealing (Eph 1:13-14), teaching (1 Cor 2:9-10), intercession (Rom 8:26-27), comfort (Jn 14:18), and empowering (Acts 1:8).

1.6. God as Preserver and Benefactor.

We depend on God and submit to him as our creator, preserver, and benefactor. Lord, we acknowledge you are God. You made us. We are your people and the sheep of your pasture (Ps 100:3), so we come to worship and bow down, kneeling before the Lord our maker (Ps 95:6-7). I praise you because I have been remarkably and wondrously made. My bones were not hidden from you when I was formed in the depths of the earth. All my days were written in your book and planned before a single one of them began (Ps 139, 14-15). Lord, I submit to you who stretched out the heavens, laid the foundations of the earth, formed and created our spirit (Zech 12:1; Jer 38:16; Heb 12:9), breathed into us life (Jb 33:4), and continue to hold our breath in your hand (Dn

5:23) until you take our breath and we return to the dust (Ps 104:29). You have placed within our hearts wisdom and understanding (Jb 38:36), more than the beasts of the earth and more than the wisdom of the birds of the heavens (Jb 35:10).

You are the potter. We are the clay and the work of your hands (Is 64:8). You brought us from the womb to feel safe in our mother's arms (Ps 22:9), so I praise you continually (Ps 71:6). In you, we live and move and exists (Acts 17:28). We cannot plan our own steps because our lives our not our own (Jer 10:23). Rather, our futures reside in your hands (Ps 31:15). Your steadfast love never ceases; your mercies never come to an end; they are new every morning; great is your faithfulness (Lam 3:22–23).

1.7. God's ownership and dominion.

We declare God to be our God and acknowledge his ownership of and dominion over us. Lord, I declare to you, you are my Master, and I have nothing good apart from you (Ps 16:2); and any good I may possess brings you nothing (Jb 35:7). Even though others have held dominion over us, we worship you alone (Is 26:13) as our blessed and only Sovereign, the King of kings and Lord of lords (1 Tim 6:15).

In response to your commands, Israel declared you to be their Lord and committed to walk in your ways (Dt 26:16-17). Similarly today, because you have caused us to be born again, to a living hope through Christ's resurrection, to an inheritance that is imperishable, undefiled, unfading, and eternally preserved (1 Pet 1:3-4), we love you (1:8) and commit to fix our hope completely on future grace while pursuing present holiness (1:13-15), conduct ourselves with fear and honor amid our earthly residence due our great redemption (1:17-18, 2:12), love one another earnestly (1:22), and long passionately for your word (2:2). You designed your people to obey in order to bring pride, glory, and honor to your name. Unlike Israel, help me to listen (Jer 13:11; 1 Pet 2:12).

I am your servant. You have loosed my bonds (Ps 116:16) and purchased me with a great price; so I am not my own (1 Cor 6:19) and offer you a sacrifice of thanksgiving.

1.8. The privilege of prayer.

We acknowledge the immense privilege in not only being admitted but also invited and encouraged to approach you in prayer. Lord, you have commanded us to utilize every form of prayer at every available opportunity. We are to be persistent in our prayers for all believers everywhere (Eph 6:18). You have directed us to devote ourselves to prayer with an alert mind and thankful heart (Col 4:2). Simply, we should pray about everything (Phil 4:6).

Through Christ, our Great High Priest, we come boldly to your throne of grace, desiring your mercy and grace amid our time of need (Heb 4:16). We confidently come to you, knowing if we ask anything, according to your will, you hear us (1 Jn 5:12-14).

You delight in our prayers (Prv 15:8). You are glorified through our praise (Ps 50:23) and more pleased with our genuine thanksgiving than our heartless adherence to your laws (Ps 69:30-31).

You have said, "seek my face," and Lord, my heart responds, "your face I will seek" (Ps 27:8). Should not a people inquire of their God (Is 8:19). Lord, to whom should we go? You have the words of eternal life (Jn 6:68).

1.9. Our unworthiness in prayer.

We express our seeming insignificance and legitimate unworthiness to draw near and speak to God. What is man that you think about him and the son of man that you care for him (Ps 8:4)? Appropriately, Solomon wondered at the possibility of you dwelling with man on earth when not even the highest heavens can contain you (2 Chr 6:18). Why would you dwell with man who is deceitful and desperately wicked (Jer 17:9)? You do not even place trust in the angels and the heavens are not absolutely pure in you sight (Jb 4:17-18, 15:15-16). However, in your rich mercy, you drew us near, we who had no hope and remained far from you. And, through the blood of Christ we now have access in one Spirit to our Father (Eph 2:4-18). Like Abraham, we are merely dust and ashes. Do not be angry when we speak to you (Gn 18:27, 30). And like Jacob, we know we are not worthy of the least of all the deeds of your steadfast love and your immense faithfulness (Gn 32:10). With the same humility as the Canaanite woman, we realize you chose to give your children's bread to us undeserving dogs (Matt 15:26-27) for you are Lord of all, bestowing your riches on all who call on you (Rom 10:12).

1.10. A humble profession of our desires.

We humbly confess our soul's longing for God as the source of true happiness, our fountain of life, and source of all good. Whom have I in heaven but you? And there is nothing on earth that I desire besides you. Even if my flesh and heart fail, you are the strength of my heart. Like the priests, who you gifted yourself rather than land as an inheritance, you alone are my inheritance and my cup of blessing (Ps 73:25-26, 16:5-

6). Amid the night of my affliction, my soul yearns for you with an expectation of you hearing and responding (Is 26:9).

As the deer pants for streams of water, so my soul pants for you, my God, the living God. When will I be able to come and be in your presence? My tears taunt me, doubting your presence, yet you send your faithful love by day and your song is with me in the night (Ps 42:1-3, 8). We come hungry and thirsty for your presence and your righteousness, expecting to be blessed and satisfied as you promised (Matt 5:6; Lk 1:53).

O God, you are my God; I earnestly search for you. My soul thirst for you; my whole body longs for you, as in a dry and weary land where there is no water. So I gaze upon you in the sanctuary, to see your power and glory. My lips will praise you because your faithful love is better than life. So I will praise you as long as I live, lifting up my hands to you in prayer (Ps 63:1-4).

1.11. Our hope and confidence in God.

We profess our faith-filled confidence in the inexhaustible sufficiency of God's power, providence, and promise. Lord, I seek refuge in you; so as you promised, let me never be disgraced. Save me by your righteousness. Be a rock of refuge for me, a mountain fortress to save me (Ps 31:1, 2; 25:3). In you alone my soul patiently waits, for from you comes salvation. You alone are my rock and salvation, my fortress. My hope comes from you (Ps 62:1-5) and in your word (Ps 119:49). When I look around and no one else stands up for me, no one provides refuge, no one cares; my weak cry finds a hearing with you, my unwavering shelter and my portion (Ps 142: 4-6). While others trust in earthly powers, we trust in you, O God (Ps 20:7) and in your steadfast love forever and ever. I will thank you forever for what you have done. I will put my hope in your name, for it is good (Ps 52:8-9).

1.12. Pleading for God's acceptance in prayer.

We appeal to God to favorably accept our weak prayers. Lord, hear my prayers. In your faithfulness listen to my plea, and in your righteousness answer me (Ps 143:1). Lord, you are my rock. I call to you. Don't be deaf to me, or I will be like those going down to the pit (Ps 28:1). You hear the young ravens when they cry and provide animals with their food (Ps 147:9). How much more should I expect you to hear your child's cry?

I love that you publicly proclaim bold promises rather than whisper in dark corners. You did not tell your people to seek you if you could not be found (Is 45:19). Israel appropriately declared, "What great nation has a god as near to them as the Lord our God is near to us whenever we call on him?" (Dt 4:7). Even more so, should I not come boldly to your throne, expecting to receive grace and mercy because I have a better and sinless high priest, namely Jesus, who has passed through the heavens (Heb 4:14-16). Christ has promised to never leave us or abandon us. Since the Lord is my helper, I have no need to be afraid (Heb 13:5-6).

Lord, I call on you; hurry to help me. Listen to my voice when I call on you. May my prayer be set before you as incense, the raising of my hands as the evening offering (Ps 141:1-2). May the light of your face shine on us (Ps 4:6). Whether we remain home in our bodies or away with you, we make it our aim to be pleasing to you (2 Cor 5:9). In Christ, be pleased with us.

1.13. The needful Spirit in prayer.

We beg to be graced with the Holy Spirit's powerful assistance in our prayers. Lord, you have promised the Holy Spirit's assistance in our prayers, for we don't know what to pray for or even how to pray. So then, we praise you because the Spirit intercedes for us with groanings imperceptible to us (Rom 8:26).

In Zechariah, you promised Israel you would pour out a spirit of grace on Israel, causing them to look on the Chosen One whom they would pierce. In his gospel, the apostle John reveals Christ to be the one who would be pierced (Jn 19:37; Rv 1:7). Therefore, we thank you for fulfilling your promise of pouring out your Spirit and ask for his ongoing work in our struggling hearts.

We have received the Spirit of adoption as sons, by whom we cry, "Abba! Father" (Rom 8:15). Send light and truth to our eyes. Let them lead us into your presence, to God our exceeding joy (Ps 13:3). Open our lips, and our mouths will declare your praise (Ps 51:15).

1.14. God's glory, our highest end in prayer.

We make God's glory our primary purpose in our prayers. Lord, you demand those who come near you to treat you as holy. You will reveal your glory before all people (Lev 10:3). There is none like you among the gods; therefore, all the nations you have made will come before you and glorify your name, because you are great and alone are God (Ps 86:9, 50:10). From you and through you and to you are all things. To you be glory forever. Amen (Rom 11:36).

1.15. Full reliance on Jesus in prayer.

We completely rely on Jesus Christ for our acceptance with God, and we come to God in his name. Lord, we desire you to hear our prayers and see our despair but not because we deserve your help but because of your mercy (Dn 9:18). We stand before you in our guilt. However, because of this guilt no one can really stand before you (Ezra 9:15). So then we draw your attention to Christ's righteousness for we know we can offer spiritual sacrifices acceptable to you through Jesus Christ (1 Pe 2:5). We appreciate the fact that while we were at one time separated from Christ without hope and without you, we have been brought near to you by Christ's blood (Eph 2:12-13). Before you alone, we stand naked and exposed, having to give an account. However, we cling to our heart's faith and our mouth's confession of Christ as Lord. Jesus, our glorious, heavenly High Priest saves to the uttermost those who draw near to you through him since he lives to make intercession for them. Therefore, we draw near to your throne of grace with confidence to receive mercy and find grace in our time of need (Heb 4:13-16, 7:25; cf. 3:6, 14; 10:23, 35; 12:12). Father, look on Christ, your anointed and our shield, in whom you are well pleased. Lord, be well pleased with us in him (Ps 84:9; Matt 3:17).

2.
CONFESSION OF SIN

2.1. The reason for our confession.

We acknowledge the great reason for our humble confession. God, I am ashamed and blush to lift my face to you, for our sins have risen higher than our heads, and our guilt has mounted up to the heavens. (Ezra 9:6). We deserve open shame because we have sinned against you. (Dn 9:8). You don't even trust the angels, and the heavens are not pure in your sight; how much less pure is a corrupt and sinful person with a thirst for wickedness (Jb 15:15–16). We are completely unworthy to even respond to you (Jb 40:4). In seeing you as King, we realize we are doomed, for each of our lips are contaminated by sin, and we live among people whose lips are contaminated by sin (Is 6:5). Hopefully, in our brokenness, we may still find hope (Lam 3:29). We fear you because we know you are a consuming fire (Heb 12:29) and no one can withstand your intense anger (Ps 76:7, 90:11). Even when we are unaware of our own guilt and our conscience is clear, that does not prove we are right or innocent (1 Cor 4:4); for you judge us and you know our hearts for you know everything (1 Jn 3:20). Like the prodigal son, we have sinned against heaven and before you and are no longer worthy of being your children (Lk 15:21).

2.2. Our humble confession of sin.

We fully embrace God's encouragement to humble ourselves and confess our sins with sorrow and shame. Lord, if you kept a record of sins, no one could stand, but you offer forgiveness so that you may be feared and revered. In you we wait, and in your word we hope; because with you there is mercy and abundant redemption (Ps 130:3-8). So then, we come to you, to the One who is high and lifted up, who inhabits eternity, and whose name is holy. We come to you knowing you desire a broken spirit and will not reject a broken and repentant heart. You restore the crushed spirit and revive the repentant heart (Is 57:15; Ps 51:17, Is 66:1-2). You have graciously reminded us we will not prosper if we cover our sin but will obtain mercy if we confess and turn from our sin (Prv 28:13). Like humble David, we will acknowledge our sin. We will not cover our iniquity. And, you will forgive. This is why all who are godly offer prayer to you at a time when you may still be found, before they are drowned in the floodwaters of judgment (Ps 32:5–6). So we confess our sins because you are faithful and just to forgive us our sins and cleanse us from all unrighteousness (1 Jn 1:8-9).

2.3. Our inherent sinfulness.

We confess and grieve our inherent sinfulness, preceded by our own sinful parents and inherent in our own depraved nature, a twisted distortion of its original purity. Lord, you made man upright and virtuous, but we have sought out many evil schemes (Eccl 7:29). Even though originally pure, Adam introduced sin into the world, and with it death. So then, death spread to everyone because, in Adam, everyone sinned (Rom 5:12, 19). Like Israel, we reside among a sinful nation, loaded down with a burden of guilt. We are evil people, corrupt children who have rejected you. We have despised you and turned our backs on you (Is 1:4). Our origin and birth derive from sinful parents. No one looked on us with pity. We were abhorred and cast out on the day of our birth, but you saw us and brought life (Eze 16:1-8). We were traitors and rebels, guilty of sin from birth, a sinner the moment our mothers conceived us (Is 48:8; Ps 51:5). Worse yet, not one of us can bring purity out of an impure person (Jb 14:4). Paul describes our original state as following the course of this world, following the prince of the power of the air, following Satan who is at work in the hearts of those who refuse to obey and follow you. We pursued the desires of our mind and body, and like the rest of mankind, we were by nature deserving of wrath (Eph 2:2-3). Everyone has rejected you. We are all morally corrupt. Not a single one of us does good (Ps 14:3).

2.4. Our natural inclination toward evil.

We grieve our natural inclination toward evil, and our profound inability toward good. We examine our heart and humbly confess the following.

2.4.1. Our blindness and inability to understand divine truth.

In our fallen nature, we walk with a darkened understanding and no ability to spiritually understand. And, without the Spirit, we remain excluded from the life of God because our ignorance and hardened hearts consider the things of the Spirit of God as foolishness (Eph 4:18; 1 Cor 2:14; Ps 82:5). Naturally, as foolish people, we consistently succeed in doing evil with no idea how to do good (Jer 4:22). Even though God speaks through several methods, we may hear and see, but we never understand (Jb 33:14; Matt 13:14).

2.4.2. Our stubborn will and refusal to obey God's commands.

As fallen men, we possess a corrupt mind which is set on the flesh, hostile to you, unwilling to submit to your law, and incapable of doing so (Rom 8:6-7). In our darkness, we have no desire to know your ways. Our hearts reject your rightful place as Lord, so we conclude there is no value in serving you or praying to you (Jb 21:14-15). We refuse to listen to you because we perceive we prosper more without you (Jer 44:16-18; cf. Zech 7:11). Often, like Solomon confessed, we hate discipline, despise correction, and refuse to listen to any teacher (Prv 5:12-13). Instead, we pursue our own desires, indulging the cravings of our flesh and mind (Eph 2:3), with a stubbornness as unbending as iron and hard as bronze (Is 48:4; cf. Zech 7:12).

2.4.3. Our wicked hearts and temporal concerns further corrupting our minds.

Lord, in observing and knowing humanity, you have declared, every thought, imagination, and inclination of our hearts to be continually evil (Gn 6:5, 8:21; Jb 15:14; Jer 17:9). As a result, our actions reflect our evil hearts, and we constantly sin and fall short of your glory (Matt 15:19; Rom 3:23; Prv 24:9). You have determined destruction and sorrow on those who devise evil plans as they lie awake at night and then rise purposing to carry them out, simply because they have the power to do so (Mic 2:1-3). What foolishness to be so easily attracted and drawn away by varied and temporal trivialities (Prv 17:24).

In our unbelieving pride and wickedness, we take no thought of you. We doubt any accountability for our actions, because we doubt your existence (Ps 10:4). Like Israel who grew proud and forgot their Rock and salvation, we ignore and reject the Creator who gave us life (Dt

32:18; Jer 2:32), choosing to rather pursue worthless idols, and in so doing, become worthless (Jer 2:5). While we may think we are building a name and legacy for ourselves, like the animals, we will die and our graves will be our eternal homes (Ps 49:11-13).

2.4.4. Our inordinate affections being placed on wrong objects and extending beyond proper bounds.

Lord, we tend to set our minds on temporal, earthly things. But, since we have been raised with Christ, we should set our minds on things above, where Christ sits in a place of honor at your right hand (Col 3:1-2). Help me to increasingly value Christ so I invest my time, finances, and effort into eternally valuable things rather than wasting all I have on things that will be destroyed and come to nothing (Matt 6:19-21).

More than merely the loss of investment, when we cherish worthless idols, we turn our backs on your steadfast love (Jon 2:8); having forsaken you, we dig cisterns for ourselves that hold no water (Jer 2:13).

Too often, like unbelievers, our minds are dominated by what we will eat, what we will drink, or what we will wear. Amid our anxiety, we overlook or forget how you have clothed the grass of the field and most certainly will care for us. So then, help us to prioritize your kingdom and your righteousness and trust you to care for our needs (Matt 6:30-33). Grant us the strength and wisdom to look on the things that are unseen rather than preoccupied with the things that are seen, for what is seen is temporal and what is unseen is eternal (2 Cor 4:18).

2.4.5. The corruption of the whole man resulting in an excessive desire for pleasure, an irrational avoidance of displeasure, and rejection of the Holy Spirit's dynamic work.

Lord, in our earthly birth, we are flesh, born from flesh, and dust, doomed to return to dust (Jn 3:6; Gn 3:19; 1 Cor 15:49). In the base, corrupt form of my flesh dwells no good thing. I possess the desire to do good but have no ability to do it. Rather, I do not do the good I want but practice the evil I do not want to do (Rom 7:18-19). Amid this battle, I understand the principle that while at times desiring good, evil has taken my heart captive (Rom 7:21-23) and so easily ensnares and entangles me (Heb 12:1).

Like sinful Judah, we are loaded down with a burden of guilt. Evil and corrupt, we have despised you. The whole head is hurt, and the whole heart is sick. From the sole of the foot even to the head, no part of me finds relief (Is 1:4-6). In our flesh, we are bent on turning away from you due our deceitful and desperately wicked hearts (Hos 11:7; Jer 17:9).

In our flesh, we consistently accept our heart's lie that more joy and satisfaction may be found in that which you have created rather than in you (Rom 1:25). We are stubborn people, continually resisting the Holy Spirit (Acts 7:51). Rather than a heart pursuing the fruit of the Spirit, we produce all forms of fleshly works. However, those who belong to Christ, have nailed their passions and desires to the cross of Christ and crucified them there (Gal 5:16-24). In so doing, you have delivered them from the corrupt body of death, and they will no longer be condemned (Rom 7:24-8:1).

2.5. Sins of omission and abandonment of duty.

We have done little towards the purpose for which God has called us in our creation, our redemption, or the means of grace inherent in Christ. Lord, you created us and redeemed us for your own glory (Is 43:7). We should strive to always bring you glory, even amid the most mundane moments (1 Cor 10:31). Additionally, you have called us to serve as witnesses of your glory as the only God and our Lord and Savior (Is 43:7-11). We are to serve as a light before others, so that they may see our good works and give glory to you (Matt 5:16). For from you and through you and to you are all things. To you be the glory both now and to the day of eternity (Rom 11:36; 2 Pet 3:18).

We consistently disappoint you rather than bring you glory. Like fig trees having been planted to bear fruit, we are consistently found empty (Lk 13:6-7). You come to the vine looking for editable grapes and find sour instead (Is 5:4). Justly, you could cut us down and throw us into the fire due our lack of fruit (Matt 3:10).

We do no good. I know what is good and even desire to do good, but I do not do good (Jas 4:17; Rom 7:18-19). Like the servant, entrusted with his master's money, I tend to hide, neglect, or selfishly benefit from the talent you gave me. Like the servant, I deserve to be cast into outer darkness (Matt 25:18, 31; Lk 16:1). Not only do I fail to do good, I often spoil good, like one dead fly in a perfumer's ointment, making a rancid smell (Eccl 9:18).

We waste the gift of wisdom. As youth, in the prime of our lives, we typically pursue folly (Prv 22:15, 17:16; Eccl 10:2, 11:10); and we end our years in vanity and with a groan, having lived in sin, with the best of our years passing in struggle and sorrow (Ps 90:8-10). Unlike the ants, who accomplish much with no leader, you have gifted us leaders and rulers, and we still stay in bed and don't adequately prepare for the future (Prv 6:7-8).

We struggle to understand and believe. While we should be adequately equipped to teach others, we still need to be taught the basic principles of your Word (Lk 24:25; Heb 5:12).

We have become proud and forgotten you. Amid your blessings, we become comfortable and begin to believe our blessings flow from our hand. Pride consumes us, and we forget you (Hoses 13:6).

2.6. Active sins of commission in thought, word, and deed.

Father, I have sinned against both heaven and you. I don't deserve to be your child (Lk 15:18). My evil heart has produced thoughts and actions that fall short of your perfect glory (Matt 12:35; Rom 3:23). While my rejection of you may appear less dramatic than Belshazzar, I far too often lift up myself against you. I praise other things that hold no real value or power. I have not honored you, in whose hand rests my breath and all my ways (Dn 5:23).

Against you, and you alone, have I sinned; I have done evil in your sight. You are right to confront me and condemn me (Ps 51:4). From my youth, I have been unspiritual, a slave to sin, breaking your law which is holy, righteous, and good (Jer 22:21; Rom 7:12-14). However, I also sin in many ways I am unable to discern. Please, forgive my hidden faults (Ps 19:12). I stumble in many ways, so much so that evil surrounds me, my iniquities overtake me, and I cannot see a way out. I have lost all courage (Jas 3:2; Ps 40:12).

2.6.1. Pride.

Lord, I have plenty of reasons to be humbled due the pride in my heart, yet I often think more highly of myself than I should. Only by your grace, with a transformed mind, will I think sensibly of myself (Rom 12:2-4). May I always remember, you are not pleased with heartless, formal worship, but rather when I act justly, love mercy, and walk humbly with you (Mic 6:8). So often, we arrogantly and foolishly rely on our own understanding rather than trust you (Prv 3:5, 28:26). We perceive any success to be from our own hands, power, and ability. As a result, our hearts tend to worship our own abilities and the means of our success (Hab 1:16). We long for our own honor rather than giving you honor (Jn 7:18). Instead of grieving over our sin like Mary Magdalene or weeping bitterly over our sins like Peter (Lk 7:38, 22:61), amid our sin, we tend to be puffed up like the Corinthians (1 Cor 5:1-2). Forgive me.

> Father, may my heart not be lifted up nor my eyes raised too high. Keep me from occupying myself with things too great and too marvelous for me. Rather, like a child with his mother, calm and quiet my soul (Ps 131:1-2).

2.6.2. Lack of self-control and rash anger.

When I lack self-control, I am like a city whose wall is broken down (Prv 25:28). My rash anger leads me to do foolish things (Prv 14:17). Like Moses, when my temper is aroused, I speak foolishly and rashly (Ps 106:33). Rather than foul language, I need to pursue only speaking in a way that builds others up. I must purpose to get rid of rage, anger, clamor, slander, and all forms of malice (Eph 4:29-31).

May I always remember, the anger of man does not produce the righteousness of God. Therefore I intend to put away all filthiness and rampant wickedness and receive with meekness the implanted word, which is able to save our souls (Jam 1:20-21).

2.6.3. Covetousness and love of the world.

Lord, unlike Paul, I am not always content in the state I find myself (Phil 4:11). Financial concerns and greed often plague and consume me (Heb 13:4). This temptation towards money lays a trap for many foolish and harmful desires which would lead to my destruction (1 Tim 6:9). You have commanded, yet I need your strength, to put to death this earthly covetous longing (Col 3:5). You commanded Israel, and you command us, to not seek great things for ourselves but rather trust you will provide all we need (Jer 45:5, Matt 6:28-31).

2.6.4. Sensuality and fleshly desires.

Lord, our flesh has shaped the outlook of our minds rather than the Spirit shaping our thinking (Rom 8:5). We have spent our years on earth in luxury, satisfying our every desire, mindless to future judgment (Jas 5:5). While we need to put on Christ, we far too often dwell on how to indulge our fleshly desires (Rom 13:14), the very desires which wage war against our souls (1 Pe 2:11). We confess, we have loved only ourselves, loving pleasure rather than loving you (2 Tim 3:4). Even amid the mundane, rather than eating and drinking for your glory (1 Cor 10:31), we eat and drink for ourselves (Zech 7:6).

2.6.5. Presumptuous security and thoughtlessness to our lack of control over changes in our world.

Lord, we push away every thought of judgment and accountability, choosing rather to mindlessly satiate ourselves with temporary comforts (Amos 6:3-7). In my self-confidence, I say, "I will never be skaken" (Ps 30:6). "Come on, let's party! Tomorrow will be just like today! We'll have everything we want!" (Is 56:12).

Jesus confronted this mindset and cautioned those who might conclude, "I have plenty of goods stored up for many years; relax, eat, drink, celebrate!" when perhaps their life would come to an end that day (Lk 12:19-21).

We often set our hope in riches and our confidence in gold rather than in the living God who richly provides us with all things for our enjoyment (1 Tim 6:17; Jb 31:23-24).

2.6.6. Fear, impatience, and sadness amid suffering, and our distrust of God and His providence.

Lord, it is not unusual for me, amid suffering, to question whether you have forgotten me or deserted me (Is 49:14). I wonder if you have rejected me or will ever be kind to me again (Ps 77:7). Often, my own foolishness causes my destruction, and I still become angry with you (Prv 19:3). In my suffering and fear, I typically compound my sin and rejection toward you. I reveal my weak faith and strength when I fail under pressure (Prv 24:10). When you correct me, I act like an untrained calf in the yoke. Help me learn from your correction and come back to you (Jer 31:18). While I may cry out, "I am cut off from the Lord," truly you do hear my cry for mercy and answer my call for help (Ps 31:22). I will receive your correction and discipline as from a loving Father (Prv 3:11-12).

2.6.7. Unkindness and injustice towards others.

Lord, forgive my indifference for those closest to me. Like Joseph's brothers, I often see the distress of others and refuse to listen or help (Gn 42:21). I choose to not pursue those things which make for peace and mutual edification (Rom 14:19), but instead judge and despise my brother, overlooking my own future judgment (Rom 14:10).

Rather than love others, I struggle with jealousy and pride. I am rude and demand my own way. I am irritable and keep record of wrongs and rejoice over the calamity of others (1 Cor 13:4-6; Prv 17:5).

Instead of thinking of ways to motivate one another to love and good works (Heb 10:24), we have become conceited and provoked one another and been jealous of each other (Gal 5:26).

How can your love be in us if we see others in need and show no compassion (1 Jn 3:17). Not only have we oppressed the poor by refusing to provide food for the hungry and shelter for the homeless, but we have hidden ourselves from our own family (Is 58:7; Jas 2:6).

If I have harmed or cheated a fellow believer, or anyone, remind me that you will weigh my actions. If I fail to know my own evil, tell me. I will stop at once (Jb 34:32).

2.6.8. Sinful speech.

Lord, woe to me for I am ruined. I am a man of unclean lips, and I live among people with unclean lips (Is 6:5). Amid my many words dwell many transgressions (Prv 10:19). While the speech of righteous people feed many, my lips have spilled foolishness and perversion (Prv 10:21, 15:2, 10:32). We use foul and abusive language, filthy and crude joking, rather than thanksgiving or that which builds up and extends grace to those hearing (Eph 4:29, 5:4). Jesus promised we would give account for every careless word we speak. By our words we will be justified or condemned (Matt 12:36-37). Lord, please don't allow my tongue to ruin me (Ps 64:8).

2.6.9. Spiritual complacency and decay.

Lord, we are spiritually complacent. We possess little fervency in our spiritual development and growth. Our service to you remains inadequate and half-hearted (Rom 12:11). We claim spiritual life. Others know us to be spiritual. Yet, our spiritual works are about to die and have been found incomplete and unfinished before you (Rv 3:2).

We have observed the winds and have not sown; have considered the clouds and have not reaped (Eccl 11:4). Like the lazy person, we avoid our duties through fanciful and creative excuses, after all, a lion may be in the street! So, why not roll back over in my bed like a door on its hinges (Prv 26:13-14).

Also, at times, while consistently performing spiritual duties, we have abandoned our first love and pursuit of you – holding to your truths but not consciously loving you (Rv 2:4). We once loved you, but our love has passed away like the morning cloud and the early dew that vanishes (Hos 6:4).

O Lord, renew my love and may my spiritual pursuits flow from that genuine love. May it never be true of me that within me lies an evil, unbelieving heart which results in my falling away (Heb 3:12).

2.7. The malignant nature and great evil in our sin.

2.7.1. The sinfulness of sin.

Lord, may I always remember sin to be a transgression of your law (1 Jn 3:4). May I see the true destructive nature of sin. You allowed the wretchedness of sin to be revealed in that sin took what was good (the Law) and brought about my condemnation to death (Rom 7:13).

Every willful act of sin declares our refusal to accept your rule over us (Lk 19:14). In our sin, we act no different than Pharaoh when he declared, "Who is the Lord that I should obey his voice" (Ex 5:2). Just like Israel, we have disobeyed, rebelled against, and turned our backs on those who declared your law. In so doing, we have committed awful blasphemies (Acts 7:51-53; Neh 9:26)

2.7.2. The foolishness of sin.

O God, you know the foolishness of my sins. My sins are not hid from you (Ps 69:5). Only due your kindness and love are we not consistently characterized as foolish, disobedient, misled, enslaved to various passions and desires, spending our lives in evil and envy, hateful and hating one another (Tit 3:3-4). I was senseless and ignorant; I was like a beast before you (Ps 73:22).

Ever since my youth, my heart has been entangled with foolishness (Prv 22:15). Little hope exists for our foolishness, for a foolish man will acquire understanding as soon as a wild donkeys colt is born a man (Jb 11:12).

Regardless our ignorant confidence, without your intervention, our foolishness leads to our destruction and eternal death (Ps 49:13).

2.7.3. The unprofitableness of sin.

Lord, when we were slaves of sin, we received no valuable fruit from the sin for which we are now ashamed. Rather, our sin produced death as its fruit (Rom 6:21). What profit do we gain if we obtain the whole world and lose our own souls (Matt 16:26).

2.7.4. The deceitfulness of sin.

Lord, I need daily encouragement, or I will be hardened by the deceitfulness of sin (Heb 3:13). Compounding the problem, I am drawn away and enticed by my own lust (Ja 1:14). The pride of my own heart deceives me. I think I'm safe in my lofty dwelling and doubt anyone could ever bring me down (Oba 3).

In the garden, Satan deceived Eve in promising life and power, yet that which promised good brought death (Gn 3:13). Similarly, Paul expected the law (God's commands) to bring life, and sin took advantage and brought death instead (Rom 7:11). Sin constantly deceives by promising something attractive of which it can never deliver and instead produces destruction and death. Sin promises freedom but makes servants of corruption (2 Pet 2:19); promises us that we will not die but rather be gods (Gn 3:4-5), and in so doing, flatters us and spreads a net for our feet (Prv 29:5).

2.7.5. The offensiveness of sin to a Holy God.

Lord, first and foremost, my sin offends and dishonors you (Ps 51:4; cf. Rom 2:23). The Old Testament prophets describe Israel's sinfulness as provoking you to bitter anger (Hos 12:14), and the product of an "offspring of evildoers" (Is 1:4). Ezekiel reveals your brokenness over "our whorish heart" that have "gone whoring after their idols" (Eze 6:9). Those who harden their hearts amid their sinfulness, put you to the test, prompting you to loath them (Ps 95:8-10).

I know, in Christ, I am freed from your wrath and eternal damnation. However, my sin still grieves your Holy Spirit (Eph 4:30; Is 63:10) and reflects a whorish, evil, hardened, enslaved life from which you have delivered me. May I never, due your immense grace, underestimate the immeasurable offense of my sin towards you.

2.7.6. Sins damage to our souls.

Lord, Adam's sin plunged each of us into spiritual slavery and death, and our ongoing sins more deeply engrain our slavery (cf. Is 50:1). Our continual pursuit of sin and rejection of you brings injury to our souls and originates in the hearts of those who love death (Prv 8:36).

Our sins have separated us from you and your attentiveness to our prayers (Is 59:2). Our sins have turned your hand of blessing away and kept good from us (Jer 5:25). By our sins, our minds and consciences have been defiled (Tit 1:15).

Our sins will bring their own punishment and shame. If I abandon you or refuse to fear you, I will find it to be an evil and bitter thing (Jer 2:19). What a fool I would have been. However, I will rejoice in your acceptance as I pursue you and your holiness (Prv 14:9).

2.8. Increasing the horror and danger of sin.

2.8.1. Increased knowledge of God and his expectations.

The more divine knowledge, the greater our sin. Lord, Jeremiah searches the streets of Jerusalem to find any who do justice and seek truth. In finding none among the poor masses, he concludes their lack of repentance flows from an ignorance of you and your justice. So, he goes to the great within the city. However, even they had "broken the yoke and burst the bonds" (Jer 5:4-5). As a result, they were all torn to pieces because their sin increased even though you had abundantly provided for them.

While increased knowledge results in increased judgment for disobedience, no one can rightly plead ignorance of your will for You have made yourself clearly known through your creation. However, we still choose to worship your creation rather than you. We refuse to acknowledge you as God, producing all forms of evil, even inventing evil. Even though we are aware of your decrees, we applaud and approve those who reject them and continually practice evil (Rom 1:19-32).

We claim to be teachers and yet have never effectively taught ourselves and still practice sins worthy of death (Rom 2:21). We profess to know God, yet our actions reveal a denial (Tit 1:16).

Lord, if we have known your will and still choose to ignore and refuse to obey, our punishment will be more severe than the one who never knew. "Much will be required of everyone who has been given much. And even more will be expected of the one who has been entrusted with more" (Lk 12:47-48).

2.8.2. Increased hypocrisy.

The severity of our sin increases the more we profess spiritual adherence while continuing in sin. Lord, you despise those who claim to be spiritual but refuse to submit to the heart of your law. Isaiah confronted Israel for having "sworn by the name of the Lord and confess the God of Israel, but not in truth or right" (Is 48:1-2). In contrast, Abraham believed and pursued righteousness. As a result, he was called a friend of God (Jam 2:23).

In the most severe woe section in Scripture, Jesus condemns the scribes and Pharisees for proclaiming to be spiritual leaders, the gatekeepers of the law, yet refusing to obey the law themselves. They claimed to be the spiritual elite, yet their actions manifest immense pride and selfishness, resulting in Jesus' strict condemnation (Mat 23). This potential hypocrisy resides in every believer. Paul exhorts the church to "let everyone who names the name of the Lord depart from iniquity" (2 Tim 2:19).

Lord, may our declarations to be a followers of Christ coincide with our speech and conduct.

2.8.3. More mercies from God.

The more mercies we have received from God, the greater our sin. Lord, you desired all creation to pay attention and learn from your dealings with your people Israel. You struck them down due their continued rebellion. The children you raised and brought up rebelled against you (Is 1:2-5). While you dispensed to the nations their inheritance, your people were your portion, yet they were a foolish and senseless people. Created and established by a loving Father, they were an unfaithful, perverse, and deceitful people (Dt 32:5-6). You punish severely when we receive your mercy with pride; however, when received with humility, you bless us all the more (2 Chro 32:25-26).

We learn from Jesus' teachings, "everyone to whom much was given, of him much will be required" (Lk 12:48). A more severe punishment comes to the servant who was given more. Ideally, the more we are forgiven, the more we are to appreciate and love (Lk 7:47).

2.8.4. Warning from God's Word and our conscience.

The severity of our sin increases the more we are confronted and warned through God's Word and our own conscience concerning the dangers of sin. Lord, following our sin, you often discipline us, but we continue turning back to our heart's desires (Is 57:17). Yet, you have cautioned, whoever remains stiff-necked, after many rebukes will suddenly be destroyed, without remedy (Prv 29:1).

O may we learn from Israel. You sent your servants the prophets time and time again saying, "don't do this detestable thing that I hate." But, they did not listen or pay attention. They did not turn from their evil or stop serving other gods. As a result, your anger was poured out on Judah and Jerusalem, and they became a ruin and desolation (Jer 44:4-6).

In pride, when we resent and reject your divine guidance, when we refuse to find rest in you or extend rest to others, you will allow our hearts and minds to perceive of your Word as meaningless gibberish and senseless babbling. As a result, we will fall backward, and be broken and snared and caught (Is 28:10-13).

May we never simply be a hearer of your Word and not a doer. May we never look into your Word as into a mirror, beholding are face, and yet turning away, forgetting what we have just seen (Jam 1:23-24).

2.8.5. Increased punishment endured due our sin.

The severity of our sin increases all the more as we fail to repent and learn from increased punishment. Lord, those whom you love you rebuke and discipline. May I earnestly receive your discipline and repent (Rv 3:19). Even though painful and unpleasant, I know you discipline me for my good, so I may share in your holiness and righteousness (Heb 12:10-11).

Like a child, I often have the propensity towards foolishness, needing the rod of discipline (Prv 22:15). May I never respond to your discipline like Israel. You struck them down, but they felt no anguish; you consumed them, but they refused to take correction. Rather, they became as hardheaded as a rock. They refused to change their ways (Jer 5:3, cf. 2 Sm 7:14). They would not turn to you who struck them or seek to be reconciled with their Lord who commands armies (Is 9:13).

When some were overthrown, like Sodom, and Gomorrah, you snatched others out of the fire like a burning stick, yet they still refused to return to you. As a result, you intended to destroy them (Amos 4:11-12).

May I quickly respond to your upraised hand, see your majesty, and act justly (Is 26:10-11).

2.8.6. Increasing promises of heightened obedience.

The severity of our sin increases with more promises and vows made of better obedience. Lord, Moses set for us a standard. If we make a vow, we need to quickly keep it, because you will require it of us. If we refrain from making a vow you will not count it against us as soon. Therefore, we must be careful to do whatever comes from our lips (Dt 23:21-23; Jer 34:18). It would be better for us to never make a vow than to make one and not keep it (Eccl 5:5).

Israel would make a covenant to obey your commands, but in disobedience, would turn back from their word. You promised to treat them like the calf they cut in two for their covenant ritual (Jer 34:18).

Unlike a dog that returns to its vomit, may I never return to a life of disobedience after having committed to follow and obey you (2 Pet 2:22). May I instead dwell in the peace you have declared rather than go back to my foolish ways (Ps 85:8).

2.9. We condemn our sins and accept our worthy punishment.

Now, O our God, what can we say after all of this? For once again we have abandoned your commands (Ezra 9:10). We know, as you have declared, "cursed is everyone who does not observe and obey all the commands written in the Book of the Law" (Gal 3:10), and that the wages of sin is death (Rom 6:23), and your wrath comes upon the sons of disobedience (Eph 5:6).

Furthermore, we know all people are without excuse and the entire world is guilty before you (Rom 3:19). The Scriptures have declared that we are all prisoners of sin (Gal 3:22). And, as a result, you could justly be angry with us to the point of destroying even the final, little remnant (Ezra 9:14), erasing our names from heaven, and pouring upon us all the curses of the covenant (Dt 29:20-21).

We understand, you would be just in declaring, "they will never enter my rest" (Ps 95:11) and, in shame, strip us naked, leaving us to die of thirst in a barren wilderness (Hos 2:3, 9), leaving us to drink only the cup of your wrath (Is 51:22).

Every time you punish us, you are just. Against you and you alone, have we greatly sinned, and you gave us what we deserve (Neh 9:33; Ps 51:4), if not far less than we deserve (Ezra 9:13).

So then, I humble myself under your mighty power, and at the right time you will lift me up in honor, casting all my anxieties on you for you care for me (1 Pet 5:6-7).

2.10. God's patience and willingness to be reconciled.

O Gracious God, we do not presume on the riches of your kindness, forbearance, and patience, knowing your kindness is meant to lead us to repentance (Rom 2:4). While some have considered your patience as evidence of you not fulfilling your promises, we know your patience is prompted by your desire for no one to perish but that all should come to repentance (2 Pet 3:9). In your grace, you do not deal with us as our sins deserve (Ps 103:10), but rather you exalt yourself by showing mercy and graciously waiting for us (Is 30:18).

At times, your patience in sentencing our evil deeds leads to our foolish hearts being more bent towards evil (Eccl 8:11). However, even amid our foolishness, you extend time for repentance (Rv 2:21). You continue to call us to return to you for you will heal our faithlessness, so we come to you, for you are the Lord our God (Jer

3:22). Certainly, we bear in mind your patience means salvation (2 Pet 3:15).

So then, we tear our hearts, not just our clothes as we return to you, for you are gracious and merciful, slow to anger, and abounding in steadfast love (Jl 2:13).

2.11. Professing shame over sin and humble reception of grace.

God, our righteousness, you exalted your son as leader and Savior to extend repentance. So then, we humbly and obediently respond to all of Scripture's calls for repentance (Matt 3:2; 2 Cor 7:10; Acts 5:31).

Thank you for revealing yourself to me. While I had heard of you, my eyes now see you. Therefore, I despise myself and repent in dust and ashes (Jb 42:5-6). O that all our heads were springs of water, our eyes fountains of tears, weeping over sin. For, those who sow in tears reap with shouts of joy! Those who go out weeping, bearing the seed for sowing, come home with shouts of joy, carrying his sheaves (Jer 9:1; Ps 126:5-6).

Our iniquities have gone over our heads, like a heavy burden, too heavy to bear (Ps 38:4). Yet, weary and heavy laden, we come to Christ who promises to give rest to our souls (Matt 11:28-29).

When we pray to you, praise your name, and turn from our sin, hear in heaven and forgive (1 Kgs 8:38). As you have promised, pour out your spirit of grace as we look on him whom we have pierced and weep bitterly (Zech 12:10). May our grief be godly grief that produces repentance rather than worldly grief that produces death (2 Cor 7:10).

May we bring forth fruit consistent with repentance and never again return to our folly (Matt 3:8; Ps 85:8), for sin no longer holds dominion over us, for we are not under the law but under grace (Rom 6:14). At times, I wander like a lost sheep. Please come and find me for I have not forgotten your commands (Ps 119:176).

3.
PETITION AND REQUESTS

By means of confession, we have opened the wounds of sin, its guilt, power, and remaining presence. We must now seek God alone for sins remedy, for healing and help. We must develop and pursue a deep, abiding affection for God's mercy. Without his mercy we are lost. With his mercy we possess high esteem, value, and happiness. Therefore, like Jacob, we must wrestle with God through prayer, for our eternal souls depend on God's mercy. By means of prayer, we do not approach God with our own prescription, for God knows us better than we know ourselves and knows what he must do. Rather, we unfold our wants and desires and then trust and rest in his wisdom and goodness. In so doing, we honor him as our protector and benefactor, and follow the way he determines for the reception of his mercy. With sincere faith we trust in and plead for his promises, knowing in Christ we are qualified to receive his favor and are confident we shall receive his mercies (Eze 36:3; Jn 6:6; Mk 11:24).

Lord, help me to know the brevity of my life and find hope only in you. Rescue me from my sin and rebellion and the resulting scorn of fools (Ps 39:4, 7-8). I come to you because you know what I long for and you hear all my sighs (Ps 38:9). And as I struggle to communicate those sighs, the Spirit helps in my weakness and intercedes with inexpressible groanings. He searches our hearts and mind and intercedes for all the saints according to the will of God (Rom 8:26-27). We desire to avoid offering empty phrases and meaningless babble because you know exactly what we need even before we ask

(Matt 6:7-8). However, we come in confidence, requesting from you in the name of Jesus Christ because you have promised that if we ask, using the name of Christ, you will receive our request (Jn 16:23-24; 1 Jn 5:14-15).

3.1. We pray for forgiveness of sins.

Lord, like the humble tax collector, who stood at a distance and dared not even look up to heaven, beating his breast, I cry out to you, "O God, be merciful to me a sinner" (Lk 18:13). Because of your unfailing love and great compassion, wipe away my sinful and rebellious transgressions which haunt me day and night. Wash away my guilt and cleanse me from my sin (Ps 51:2-3). If you cleanse me, I will be pure, whiter than the snow. Please, hide your face from my sin. (Ps 51:7,9). I rejoice because Christ has mediated a better covenant, one through which you put your law on my mind and heart, and in so doing will be merciful toward my sin and will remember my sin no more (Heb 8:6-12 quoting Jer 31:31-34). That which the law of Moses could not do (Acts 13:39), Jesus Christ accomplished in his death, and in so doing gifted our justification and redemption (Rom 3:23-25). Left in my sin, my iniquity would ruin me (Eze 18:30), leading to eternal death (2 Sm 12:13; Rv 2:11). On my own, I could never stand before you, justified (Ps 143:2). But because of Christ, your anger is turned away from me and I find mercy (Hos 14:2-4). Though my sins are like scarlet, you will a make them white as snow; though they are red like crimson, you will make them white as wool (Is 1:18).

Amid our request for forgiveness, we appeal to God based on his many promises, through which our faith is encouraged and our passion in prayer increased.

3.1.1. God's infinite goodness.

For his own sake, his own glory, God unfolds his infinite goodness and eagerness to forgive. Father of compassion and God of all comfort, you are good and forgiving, rich in faithful love to all who call on You (Ps 86:5). You, Lord, are merciful and gracious, slow to anger and abounding in love and faithfulness (Ps 86:15).

Even when your people refused to obey and did not remember your miraculous works and rebelled against your leadership, you remained ready to forgive. You were slow to anger and did not forsake them (Neh 9:17).

You continue to extend kindness to a people who refuse to call on you and weary you with their disobedience. They refuse to honor you or offer appropriate sacrifice. They have been a burden and have wearied you with their iniquities. Yet for your own sake, you blot out their transgressions and remember their sins no more. You have redeemed them and called them by name; therefore, you will be with them, and nothing shall overwhelm them (Is 43).

So then, pardon the iniquity of your people, according to your greatness and your steadfast love (Num 14:17-19). There is no other like you, pardoning iniquity and passing over the rebellion of those who remain among your people. You do not remain angry forever, but delight in showing unchanging love. You will again have compassion on us. You will tread our iniquities. You will hurl our sins into the depths of the sea (Mic 7:18-19).

3.1.2. Christ's righteousness.

We rely solely on Jesus Christ's merit and righteousness as the grounds for requesting forgiveness of sins. O Holy God, not only are you a good and compassionate God but also a righteous God who loves righteous deeds (Ps 11:7) and will by no means leave the guilty unpunished (Ex 34:7). We could never reasonably plead, "have patience with me, and I will repay you everything" (Matt 18:26), for all of us are unclean. Our righteous deeds are like filthy rags (Is 64:6). But, gloriously, you have united us with Christ Jesus, who is our righteousness and redemption (1 Cor 1:30). You made him who knew no sin to be sin for us, so that in him we might become the righteousness of God (2 Cor 5:21, cf. 1 Jn 2:1-2).

Who then can be against us? In order to show your righteousness, you delivered up your own Son for us all. No one can charge us for you are the God who justifies. No one can condemn us for Christ Jesus is the one who died, who was raised to the right hand of God, and intercedes for us (Rom 8:31-34, 3:25).

So then, because of what Christ has done, I consider as worthless any good deeds I may have offered – indeed I consider everything as loss and rubbish due the surpassing worth of knowing Christ Jesus my Lord. I now possess the righteousness from you that comes only through faith in Christ (Phil 3:7-9).

3.1.3. God's promises.

Throughout His Word, God has promised to forgive all who truly repent and believe the gospel. Our Father, who forgives, you have called us to forsake our ways and our unrighteous thoughts. You have called us to return to you, so that you may have compassion on us, be our God, and abundantly pardon (Is 55:7). For to you belong mercy and forgiveness (Dn 9:9).

Lord, we know, if you were to mark iniquities, no one could stand. However, with you there is forgiveness that you may be feared (Ps 130:3-4).

In your new covenant, you promised a Deliverer who would banish ungodliness and take away sins (Rom 11:25), who would forgive iniquity and remember our sins no more (Jer 31:34).

You have promised that if we confess our sins, you are faithful and just to forgive us our sins and to cleanse us from all unrighteousness (1 Jn 1:9).

Along with the apostles, we praise you for one of the primary benefits of Christ's work being the forgiveness of sin (Acts 2:28, 3:19, 4:12, 5:31, 10:43, 13:38-39; 1 Thes 1:10; 1 Cor 15:3). We have redemption through Christ's blood, the forgiveness of sins (Eph 1:7).

Gloriously, due to Christ's work, you have removed our sins from us, as far as the east is from the west (Ps 103:12).

3.1.4. Our own sin.

Our passionate request for forgiveness flows from our own misery and danger because of sin. For the sake of your own reputation, O Lord, forgive my sin; for it is great (Ps 25:11). Because of your goodness, do not remember the sins of my youth; rather, according to your lovingkindness, remember me (Ps 25:7). Preserve me with your lovingkindness, for evils without number surround me. My sins pile up so high, I cannot see my way out. My heart fails me, and courage leaves me. Lord, be pleased to deliver me and quickly come to my aid (Ps 40:11-13; cf. Ps 78:8-9). Let your compassion quickly meet our needs, for we are on the brink of despair (Ps 78:8).

3.1.5. Our blessed condition.

Our faith is encouraged amid our requests for forgiveness due the blessed condition of those who are forgiven. Father of all mercies, when I refuse to confess my sin, my whole body wastes away and groans all day long. However, you extend joy to me when my sin is uncovered, my transgressions are forgiven, and no charge is laid against my sin (Ps 32:1-3).

I rejoice and praise you for the redemption and forgiveness I have received through Christ's blood. You have showered me with the riches of your grace. You have magnificently displayed your wisdom in displaying the mystery of your will (Eph 1:7-8). As a result, in Christ, I am no longer condemned. You have set me free (Rom 8:1). Having been forgiven much, we love much and proceed in peace (Lk 7:47, 50).

3.2. We pray for reconciliation.

We pray God reconciles us to himself, obtaining his favor, blessing, and gracious acceptance.

3.2.1. Peace with God.

We desire to live at peace with God having his anger turned away from us. O God of peace, you have declared us righteous by faith and given us peace with you through our Lord Jesus Christ. Through Christ, we undeservedly stand before you and boast in your glory and stand in awe of your radiant holiness (Rom 5:1-2).

Having given us peace, Lord, don't become a terror to us. You are my refuge in the day of disaster (Jer 17:17). Revive us so your people can rejoice in you. Show us your unfailing love, O Lord, and grant us your salvation (Ps 85:5-7).

We were far away from you, but now, having been united in Christ Jesus, we have been brought near through the blood of Christ. He is our peace. You united Jew and Gentile, in one body, so you could reconcile both to you through the cross, through which the hostility was put to death. So we are no longer foreigners or strangers, but fellow citizens with the saints, and members of God's household (Eph 2:13-16,19).

3.2.2. Covenanted with God.

Undeserving, we place our eternal hope in being admitted into the new covenant relationship with God. Our faithful God, I praise you for a better covenant. Even Moses, the mediator of the old covenant spoke of a better covenant. He longed for the day when Israel would have a mind that understands and eyes to see (Dt 29:4). Through Jeremiah, you promised a new and better covenant, one in which you would place the law within us, write it on our hearts, and be our God (Jer 31:31-33). You promised to give a new heart, and place your Spirit within us, and remove our hearts of stone, so that we may obey you (Eze 36:26-27).

While you declared the new covenant to Israel, you additionally included those who were far off. In union with Christ, we Gentiles, who were far away from you have been brought near, into the blessings of the new covenant (Eph 2:13-14).

Through faith, we hope in Christ, who has fulfilled the law and brought an end to the law's sacrifices through his own blood. Through faith in Christ, the Spirit of Christ dwells within us (Rom 8:9-11), and we have received the promise of an eternal inheritance, enjoying a permanent, unbroken relationship with you (Heb 9:15).

3.2.3. Favor with God.

We desire God's favor and a portion of his saving love. God of mercy, I have sought your favor with all my heart. Be gracious to me according to your promise (Ps 119:58), for your favor lasts a lifetime (Ps 30:5). Your unfailing love is better than life itself, so I praise you (Ps 63:3)! Lord, make your face shine upon me, and be gracious to me. Look on me with favor and give me peace (Num 6:25-26).

Remember me, O Lord, when you show favor to your people. Pay attention to me when you deliver, so that I may enjoy the prosperity of your chosen ones, rejoice in the joy of your nation, and boast along with the people who belong to you (Ps 106:4-5).

3.2.4. Blessings of God.

We long for God's blessing, promised to Abraham, received in Christ. O God, Lord and Creator of heaven and earth, be gracious to us and bless us. Look on us with favor, revealing your salvation throughout the nations (Ps 67:1-2, 134:3).

Like Esau, may we cry out to you for blessing (Gn 27:38). May we like Jacob tenaciously cling to you until we receive your blessing (Gn

32:26), for we know, in your presence, we find ultimate blessing, life forevermore (Ps 133:3, 134:3, 1 Chr 17:27).

We praise you, Father of our Lord Jesus Christ, for in Christ you have blessed us with every spiritual blessing in the heavens (Eph 1:3). We praise you, for the blessing of Abraham has come to us Gentiles, and through faith, we have received the promised Spirit (Gal 3:13).

3.2.5. Presence of God.

We desire God's presence among us. Jehovah Shammah (Eze 48:35), having found favor with you in Christ, I pray, do not lead me anywhere where your presence will not go with me (Ex 33:13-14), for you have promised to never leave us or forsake us (Heb 13:5).

Do not cast me from your presence or take your Holy Spirit from me (Ps 51:11). May I always dwell along with the upright in your presence, giving you thanks (Ps 140:13).

3.2.6. A sense of reconciliation.

We pray we may experience evidence of God's reconciliation and acceptance. Not only do we desire to be pardoned, but as well desire to sense or experience our pardon for sin and our adoption. We want to feel pardoned. Our healing God, you have cleansed me in Christ. Now, make me to hear joy and gladness, so that the bones you have crushed may rejoice (Ps 51:7-8). Tell my soul, "You are my salvation" (Ps 35:33). Command my heart to rejoice because my sins are forgiven (Matt 9:2).

Through the perfect, atoning Christ, may I experience the cleansing of my conscience from dead works, so that I may serve you, the living God (Heb 9:14).

Instead of receiving the spirit of slavery leading to fear, you have granted us the Spirit of adoption, by whom we cry, "Abba! Father!" The Spirit himself bears witness with our spirit that we are children of God (Rom 8:15-16).

— *We petition God for a substantive peace within our conscience and a sense of security flowing from our justification.* Lord of peace, give us peace at all times (2 Thes 3:16), and may your peace, which surpasses all understanding, guard our hearts and minds through Christ Jesus (Phil 4:7), and may this peace rule in our hearts and guide our treatment of one another in the body of Christ (Col 3:15).

You have left your Spirit of peace with us, a peace that the world cannot give. So then, let our hearts be free from distress and fear (Jn 14:27). May the effect of the Spirit's work of righteousness be peace, quietness, and confidence (Is 32:17).

We will listen to what you say, for you speak peace to your people, your faithful servants, so keep us from turning to folly (Ps 85:8).

Now, O great God of hope, fill us with all joy and peace as we believe in Christ, so that we may overflow with confident hope through the power of the Holy Spirit (Rom 15:13).

3.3. We pray for God's grace.

We pray for God's grace and the powerful and practical impact of that grace operating on us. God of grace, we draw near your throne, through our sympathetic high priest, so that we may receive mercy and find grace to help in time of need (Heb 4:15-16). In your good pleasure you have made all goodness to dwell in Christ, and from this abundance, we have received one gracious gift after another (Col 1:19; Jn 1:16).

3.3.1. Grace to fight.

We pray for strength to combat every evil thought, word and deed. Having been removed from the guilt of sin, we as well desire freedom from the power of sin, the control of our fleshly desires, and the power to overcome Satan's temptations.

Thank you God! Under the law, we once were slaves to sin. But now, sin is no longer our master. The Spirit of Christ has set us free from sin and death. Now under grace, we are slaves of righteousness who obey from the heart (Rom 6:14, 17, 8:2).

May we walk by the Spirit, no longer gratifying the desires of our flesh, for we belong to Christ and have crucified the flesh with its passions and desires (Gal 5:16, 24).

Give us grace to put off our sinful nature, corrupted by deceitful desires, and put on our new nature, created according to God's likeness in righteousness and holiness (Eph 4:22, 24).

Through the cross of Jesus Christ, may the world be crucified to us, and we to the world (Gal 6:14).

— *And that Satan's temptations may not overcome us.* O Lord, although my spirit is willing, my flesh is so weak. Empower me to continually pray that I may not enter into temptation (Matt 26:41). However, I know no temptation has overtaken me that is not common to mankind, yet you have promised to be faithful and will not allow me to be tempted beyond what I am able and will provide a means of escape so I may endure (1 Cor 10:13).

I commit to putting on the full armor of God so I may stand against the devil's schemes. Remind me our battle is not against flesh-and-blood enemies but against evil rulers and unseen authorities and evil spirits in heavenly places. In order to stand firm, I clothe myself with truth, righteousness, the gospel of peace, faith, salvation, and God's Word (Eph 6:11-17).

My primary means of resisting the devil and causing him to flee comes in submission to you (Jas 4:7). Firm in the faith, I commit to continually resisting him, encouraged by the fact that I'm not alone in this battle (1 Pet 5:9). Gloriously, you will soon crush Satan under our feet (Rom 16:20).

3.3.2. Grace to equip.

We pray for grace to equip us for every good thought, word, and deed. We pray we are kept from sin but also that we may always be and do all you require of us. Our wise God, because of you, we are in Christ Jesus, who became God-given wisdom for us – our righteousness, sanctification, and redemption (1 Cor 1:30). We have been joined with him in the likeness of his death and will certainly also be in the likeness of his resurrection. Therefore, for your glory, may we live in newness of life (Rom 6:5, 4).

— *Grace newly initiated. We pray God initiates saving grace within those who have yet to experience it.* O merciful God, restore to me the joy of my salvation so that I teach transgressors your ways and sinners are restored to you (Ps 51:12-13). May we, like John the Baptist, be used by the Spirit to turn the lost to you and the disobedient to the attitude of the righteous (Lk 1:17).

Prompted by your mercy and love, may you make alive in Christ those who are dead in their transgressions and sins (Eph 2:4-5). Declare,

"Live! Be mine!" (Eze 16:6, 8). Open their eyes so they may turn from darkness to light and from the power of Satan to God, that by faith in Christ they may receive forgiveness of sins and share among those who are sanctified (Acts 26:18).

May the Word of God demolish strongholds and every proud thing that is raised up against the knowledge of God, and let every thought be captive to the obedience of Christ (2 Cor 10:4-5).

— *Grace continued and perfected. We pray God graciously continues the work he initiated and will at length perfect.* O, Jehovah M'Kaddesh, for your glory, may you make me worthy of your calling and fulfill every resolve for good and every work of faith by Christ's power (1 Thes 1:11). Based on your promises, I trust you will finish the work in us you began and will complete until Christ's return (Phil 1:6). O Lord, motivated by your steadfast love, fulfill the purpose you have established for us. Do not abandon those whom you have given to Christ (Ps 138:8; Jn 6:37). Lord, assuredly, in our weakness, your grace is sufficient for your power is made perfect in our weakness (2 Cor 12:9-10). Therefore, we will be strong in you and in the strength of your might (Eph 6:9).

3.3.3. Grace to teach and instruct.

We request the work of the Spirit in teaching and instructing us, so that we are both knowledgeable and intelligent in the things of God. My all-knowing Father, may I cry out for knowledge and lift up my voice for understanding. May I seek it as silver and search for it as for hid treasure. In so doing, you have promised I would find the fear of the Lord and the knowledge of God (Prv 2:3-5). Open my eyes so I may see marvelous truths in your instructions (Ps 119:18). In pressing on to know you, you will come to us as certain as the appearance of the dawn and like spring rains that water the earth (Hos 6:3), from the least of us to even the greatest (Heb 8:11). In knowing you, the only true God, and Jesus Christ whom you have sent, we possess eternal life (Jn 17:3).

O great Father of glory, give your Spirit, of wisdom and revelation so we may grow in our knowledge of you. May the eyes of our hearts be enlightened so we may know the hope of your calling, the wealth of your glorious inheritance in the saints, and the immeasurable greatness of your power toward us who believe (Eph 1:17-20), so that we may reach all the riches of full assurance of understanding and the knowledge of God's mystery, which is Christ (Col 2:2)

3.3.4. Grace to lead, keep, and correct in truth.

Great God and omniscient Father, may your Spirit come and guide us into all truth (Jn 16:13), making us understand how we've gone astray (Jb 6:24). Teach us what we cannot see (Jb 34:32), so we may hold fast to that which is good (1 Thes 5:21).

Lord, help us mature, so we are no longer children, tossed about by every wave and wind of doctrine or the appealing lies of deceitful people. Rather, speaking the truth in love, may we grow up into Christ, who is our head (Eph 4:14-15). May we possess the discernment to know whether teachings are from you, and in knowing the truth be made truly free (Jn 7:17, 8:36). May we hold on to the pattern of sound teaching we have learned and trust – a pattern shaped by faith and love in Christ Jesus (2 Tim 1:13, 3:14).

3.3.5. Grace to help our memories.

We pray for a healthy memory allowing God's truths to be readily accessible when needed. O Holy Spirit, our Great Comforter, remind us of all things (Jn 14:26), so our lives may be filled with the rich message of Christ (Col 3:16). Cause us to listen carefully so we may not drift away from the truth (Heb 2:1). Empower us to be competent in the use of the Scriptures so that we may be complete, equipped for every good work, (2 Tim 3:17) bringing out new and old treasures from its truths (Matt 13:52).

3.3.6. Grace to direct our consciences.

We request the Spirit to reveal our duty and make us wise, knowing, and judicious Christians. Lord and source of all wisdom, give your servant an understanding and discerning mind (1 Ki 3:9; Prv 14:8), so when accompanied by love, we may be able to discern what is excellent. In so doing, may we walk in a worthy manner, pure and blameless for the day of Christ, filled with the fruit of righteousness coming from Jesus Christ (Phil 1:9-11; Col 1:9-10).

When we do not know what to do, we will focus our eyes on you (2 Chro 20:12). In so doing, may we hear your word behind us, saying, "This is the way, walk in it" (Is 30:21). Direct my steps according to your word; let no sin rule over me (Ps 119:133).

3.4. We pray for God's work of sanctification.

Our sinfulness necessitates the Holy Spirit root within us biblical truth and holy character. Faithful God, you have called me to yourself, and I rest assuredly in knowing you will make me completely holy and preserve my spirit, soul, and body blameless until Christ's return (1 Thes 5:23-

24). In anticipation of that moment, create in me a clean heart, and renew a steadfast spirit within me. Do not banish me from your presence or take your Spirit from me. Restore to me the joy of your salvation and grant me a willing spirit (Ps 51:10-12).

You have promised to put your law in my mind and inscribe it on my heart (Heb 8:10). In so doing, may I, in my inner being, delight to do your will (Ps 40:8; Rom 7:22).

Having been a slave to sin, through the Spirit's work, I obey from my heart the teachings that have claimed my allegiance and affections (Rom 6:17). Therefore, may I not be conformed to this world and the passions of my former ignorance but transformed by the renewing of my mind so that I may be holy in all my conduct (1 Pe 1:14-15).

3.4.1. Faith.

My Father and provider, for Christ's sake and as a gift, you granted me saving faith (Phil 1:29; Eph 2:8). Now, having been crucified with Christ, who loves me and gave himself for me, I live in this fleshly body by faith in him (Gal 2:20). So then, in harmony with the apostles, "increase my faith" (Lk 17:5). Establish and strengthen my faith so I may walk in Christ, overflowing with gratitude (Col 2:6-7). In the face of unbelief, may my faith not waiver concerning your promises (Rom 4:20). Produce in me a faith which is an assurance of things hoped for and a conviction of things not seen (Heb 11:1). May my eyes be ever towards you (Ps 25:15, 16:8), enduring as if I see the invisible and looking to the eternal (Heb 11:26-27). [Henry Law offers a great prayer for faith in Family Prayers, Week One, Tuesday Morning.]

3.4.2. Fear of God.

Lord, work in us that fear of you, which is the beginning of wisdom (Prv 1:7), the instruction in wisdom (Prv 15:33), and a fountain of life (Prv 14:27). Put your fear in our hearts so that we never turn away from you (Jer 32:40). May our hearts be united in a fear of you rather than consumed by and fragmented over temporal concerns (Ps 86:11), so that we may obey your commands which is our whole duty (Eccl 12:13). Do not let our hearts envy sinners; but instead, always fear you (Prv 23:17).

3.4.3. Love of God rather than the world.

Lord, we need your grace to love you with all our heart, soul, mind, and strength (Matt 22:37). We need you to cleanse our hearts, and our children's hearts, so we may love you with all our mind and being – and live (Dt 30:6). So then, may the Holy Spirit whom you have given, pour your love into our hearts (Rom 5:5). Though we have not seen you, we love you; and in believing, we possess joy that is inexpressible and filled with glory (1 Pe 1:8). May Christ's love control us, and may we no longer live for ourselves but for him who died and rose again (2 Cor 5:14-15). May we love you and set our minds on you, rather than the world or the things in the world (1 Jn 2:15; Col 3:2).

3.4.4. Tender conscience and life of repentance.

O Lord, my Creator, remove this stony, stubborn heart and give me a heart of flesh, a tender and responsive heart (Eze 11:19). May I live a life of love that flows from a pure heart and a good conscience and a sincere faith (1 Tim 1:5). I desire to be sensitive to the Spirit's conviction and wise to Satan's designs, as to not be outwitted by Satan

(2 Cor 2:11) and avoid sin in all its varied forms (1 Thes 5:22). Help me avoid the pride which prompts me to think I can fight this battle alone, for in that pride I will fall (1 Cor 10:12). So then, when I sin, may I be quick to confess my sins, reassured of your quickness to forgive and cleanse me from all unrighteousness (1 Jn 1:9).

3.4.5. Love of others.

Loving Father, you have taught us to love (1 Thes 4:9-10). Please, develop within us a sincere and deep love for others (1 Pet 1:22), a love that binds everything together in perfect harmony (Col 3:14), a love that preserves unity of the Spirit through the bond of peace (Eph 4:3), a love that results in God's presence among us (2 Cor 13:11). And may we love our neighbors, and in so doing, fulfill the law (Rom 13:9-10) and reveal to the world we truly are your disciples (Jn 13:35).

May we do good and live peaceably with all people, especially to those who belong to the family of believers (Rom 12:18; Gal 6:10), understanding we must actively pursue the things which make for peace and mutual edification (Rom 14:19).

Empower us to love our enemies and pray for those who persecute us (Matt 5:44). May we be patient with others and quick to forgive, motivated by gratitude for the forgiveness we possess in Christ (Col 3:13).

3.4.6. Self-denial.

Lord, daily give us grace to deny ourselves, take up our cross, and follow Christ (Matt 16:24). May we not be motivated by love of self (2 Tim 3:2) but rather the good of others (1 Cor 10:24). May we not be led by our own wisdom and understanding, but rather fear the Lord and turn from evil (Prv 3:5, 7). May we not be consumed with the desires of our flesh (1 Jn 2:16) but rather keep our bodies under control (1 Cor 9:27). Grant that we live not to ourselves or die to ourselves, but rather whether we live or die, may we live for you (Rom 14:7-8).

3.4.7. Humility and meekness.

My Savior, on whom I have rested my weary soul, may I learn from you to be gentle and lowly in heart (Matt 11:29). May I reflect your mind, not looking to my own interests but rather the interests of others (Phil 2:4-5). Hide pride from me. Instead, clothe me in humility and a gentle and quiet spirit, which you value (1 Pe 5:5, 3:4).

Lord, give me grace to live my life in a manner worthy of your calling, humble, gentle, and patient, bearing with others in love (Eph 4:1-2). May I slander no one, but be peaceable and considerate, and gentle towards all people (Tit 3:2-3).

So, as chosen by you, holy, and beloved, I purpose to put on a heart of compassion, kindness, humility, gentleness, and patience (Col 3:12). You have been merciful to me, so I will strive to be merciful to others (Lk 6:36).

3.4.8. Contentment.

God, my provider, graciously gift me with the wealth of godliness accompanied by contentment (1 Tim 6:6). May your unending presence and care for me result in contentment and a deterrence from a life consumed by money (Heb 13:5). Teach me to be content in any and every situation, in need or in abundance, hungry or well fed (Phil 4:11-12) — remembering little with the fear of the Lord is better than great wealth with trouble (Prv 15:16) — remembering amid my contentment, your grace overflows sufficient for both me and my good deeds towards others (2 Cor 9:8).

3.4.9. Hope in God, Christ, and eternal life.

Lord, you strengthen my hope of salvation through the encouragement of your Word and the development of my character through suffering. I'm so thankful this hope will not lead to disappointment for I know you dearly love me as evidenced by the Holy Spirit filling my heart with your love (Rom 5:4-5, 15:4).

My joy roots its certainty in the truth that you are my helper. You, Lord God, are my hope (Ps 146:5). I praise you for in your great mercy you have given me new birth into a living hope through Jesus' resurrection from the dead (1 Pe 1:3), and may that hope be a sure and steadfast anchor for my soul, anchored in the inner place behind the veil where Christ eternally intercedes for me (Heb 6:19-20). Empower me to diligently hold to the full assurance of hope until the end (Heb 6:11).

3.4.10. Preservation from sin.

Most Holy Lord, turn my eyes from looking at worthless things (Ps 119:37). Keep me from paths which promise life and satisfaction but offer destruction and grief (Ps 119:29). Turn my heart from the seduction of evil, leading me to participate in sin alongside others who behave wickedly (Ps 141:4). Keep me from deliberate sins. Do not let them rule over me. Additionally, forgive my hidden faults, for I cannot know all the sins lurking in my heart (Ps 19:13,12).

May your grace be sufficient, ready, and mighty. Please, never give me over to my own stubborn heart and allow me to follow my own counsel (Ps 81:12).

May I treasure your Word in order to avoid sinning against you (Ps 119:11) Therefore, preserve my life according to your Word (Ps 119:37).

May I live a clean and innocent life as your child (Ps 18:23) in order to shine as a light in a crooked and perverse society (Phil 2:15) giving no grounds for the world to blaspheme the noble name of Jesus Christ (Jam 2:7). Help me to live carefully – not as a fool but as wise (Eph 5:15), and in so doing, put to silence the ignorance of foolish people (1 Pe 2:15) and adorn the doctrine of God my Savior in all things (Tit 2:10).

3.4.11. Control and good use of the tongue.

Lord, I'm committed to watching what I am doing and not sin in what I say (Ps 39:1). I intend to not be rash with my speech. Therefore, I am determined to speak less and more carefully (Eccl 5:2). However, at times in my silence, my mind and heart burn within me and I speak

(Ps 39:2-3). In fact, we all make many mistakes in our speech. If we could control our tongues, we would be perfect (Jam 3:2). So please set a guard over my mouth and watch over the door of my lips (Ps 141:2).

Lord, may my speech always be gracious, seasoned with salt, so I know how to appropriately respond to others with wisdom and justice (Col 4:5; Ps 37:30), with the teaching of kindness on my tongue (Prv 31:26).

3.4.12. Strength to live a godly life.

O Spirit of truth, by your grace, teach me to deny ungodliness and worldly lusts and to live in a sensible, righteous, and godly way as I eagerly wait the return of Christ, who offered himself in order to redeem us from all lawlessness and to cleanse a people for his own possession, eager to do good works (Tit 2:11-14).

—*Thoughtful and careful.* Lord, you directed me to come to you and ask if I lack wisdom. You have promised to liberally give me wisdom without rebuking or criticizing me (Jam 1:5). I desperately need the shrewdness of a serpent for I live in a world full of wolves. However, like the innocence of a dove (Matt 10:16), may your wisdom brighten my face and soften its sternness (Eccl 8:1). Help me to make the most of every opportunity, living wisely among unbelievers (Col 4:5) and live with integrity in my own home (Ps 101:2).

— *Honest and sincere.* Lord, I desire to conduct myself with sincerity and purity — manifestations of your wisdom (2 Cor 1:12). Your wisdom is not jealous and selfish. Jealousy and selfish ambition, which are earthly, natural, and demonic, produce disorder and every kind of evil. Instead, your wisdom is pure, peaceable, gentle, reasonable, full of mercy and good fruit, impartial, and sincere (Jam 3:15-17). Let integrity and godliness protect me, for I put my hope in you (Ps 25:21).

— *Active and diligent.* Lord, you have given us tasks for each day, whether they be for the advancement of your kingdom, our own spiritual and physical care, or the care of our families and communities. Empower us to do the work each day requires (Ezra 3:4), with diligence and a desire to serve you (Rom 12:11) and not man (Col 3:23), making the best use of our time because the days are evil and you will be returning soon (Eph 5:16). I desire that you find me faithfully serving when you return (Lk 12:43). To that end, may I remain steadfast, immovable, always abounding in the work of the Lord, for we know our efforts for the Lord are not in vain (1 Cor 15:58).

— *Unwavering and courageous.* Lord, teach me to endure hardship as a good soldier of Jesus Christ (2 Tim 2:3); fearless amid the reproach of others and unbroken by their taunts and insults (Is 51:7). May I never be ashamed of you and your truths in this adulterous and sinful generation (Mk 8:37).

Even if the Spirit were to warn me that imprisonment and persecution awaited me everywhere, may I consider my life of no value to myself, so that I may finish my course with joy (Acts 20:23-24).

In everything, may I present myself as a true minister of God, patiently enduring troubles, hardships, and distress of every kind. May I prove my purity through understanding, patience, and kindness, empowered by the Holy Spirit, accompanied with sincere love. May I faithfully preach the truth, strengthened by your power (2 Cor 6:4, 6-7). So then, for me, it matters little whether I am judged by any human authority. I don't trust my own judgment, but rather fear and rest in the judgment of the Lord (1 Cor 4:3-4).

— *Pleasant and cheerful.* Lord, enable me to always rejoice in you (1 Thes 5:16; Phil 4:4). May the work of the Spirit and the words of your mouth produce joy and singing in my life (Acts 8:39; Ps 138:5). May my cheerful heart act as a good medicine to those around me (Prv 17:22). May my satisfaction amid abundance and comfort never result in a failure to serve you in joy and gladness of heart (Dt 28:47), and deliver me from the heaviness of heart that weighs a person down (Prv 12:25).

3.4.13. Wisdom and maturity.

God, our provider and head, we will only grow in grace and knowledge of Jesus Christ as you nourish and develop us (Col 2:19; 2 Pe 3:18). May we more and more be like a refreshing dew from heaven and like a lily that spreads its roots like a cedar of Lebanon (Hos 14:5-6). Help me to grow in righteousness – like the glimmer of dawn, growing brighter and brighter until the full light of day (Prv 4:18). I have not obtained maturity nor am I perfect, but I strive to lay hold of the perfection and righteousness for which Christ laid hold of me. So then, I forget all that lies behind, and I reach forward to what lies ahead – the goal – the prize of the upward call of God in Jesus Christ (Phil 3:12-14).

3.5. We pray for future grace.

With sincere faith, we pray for God's future grace. We trust in and plead for his promises, knowing in Christ we are qualified to receive his favor and are confident we shall receive his mercies

3.5.1. Support and comfort in suffering.

Father of compassion and God of all comfort, we were born for trouble as surely as the sparks fly upward (Jb 5:7). So then eternal God, be my dwelling place, my refuge. I rest in your everlasting arms (Dt 33:27). Amid suffering, I will strive to shout for joy and sing praises to your name because you have redeemed me (Ps 71:23). May your truths be the song of my life and the joy of my heart (Ps 119:54, 111). We pray that we will be strengthened with your glorious might so we will have all the endurance and patience we need (Col 1:11). We are hard pressed on every side, but not crushed; perplexed, but not driven to despair (2 Cor 4:8); sorrowful, but always rejoicing; poor, but making many rich; having nothing, but possessing everything (2 Cor 6:10).

3.5.2. Preservation until the end.

Oh, glorious and faithful God, who can keep me from stumbling, you have promised to deliver me from every evil and bring me safely into your heavenly kingdom. Until our glorious reunion, make our love for others grow and overflow so that our hearts may be blameless and holy before your glorious presence (Jd 24; 2 Tim 4:18; 1 Thes 3:12-13). May we build each other up in our faith, keeping ourselves in the love of God as we wait for the mercy of our Lord Jesus Christ (Jd 20-21).

Like Peter, if Satan demands to sift me, may Christ intercede on my behalf, so my faith does not fail (Lk 22:31-32). Honor Christ's request to protect me from the evil one. Perfect me through your truth (Jn 17:15, 17). Grant that I call on you as long as I live because you bend down to hear my cries of mercy (Ps 116:2). Empowered by your Spirit, I will pursue my integrity and increasing righteousness until I die. Ultimately, I will cling to Christ's righteousness, never letting go (Jb 27:5-6).

3.5.3. Preparation for death.

Eternal Father, remind me of my mortality and the brevity of life. My days are a handbreadth. My entire lifetime is nothing to you. At best, I am just a breath (Ps 39:4-5). My days on earth merely cast a passing shadow as I dwell here momentarily as a foreigner and stranger in this land (1 Chro 29:15). I desire to consistently live with this perspective so that I may gain a heart of wisdom (Ps 90:12; Dt 32:29). Lord, I don't know when Christ will return, so I stay dressed for action with my lamp burning, waiting for my master's return (Lk 12:35-40).

I will praise you if I come to the grave at a ripe old age as grain harvested at the proper time (Jb 5:26); and I will praise you if I die young, for to be absent from the body is to be present with my Lord (2 Cor 5:8). Regardless the moment, walk with me through the valley of the shadow of death so I fear no evil. Comfort me with your presence (Ps 23:4). Let goodness and mercy follow me all my days until you redeem my life, snatch me from the power of the grave, and receive me to glory where I will dwell in your house forever (Ps 23:6, 49:15, 73:24).

3.5.4. Fit for heaven.

Lord, we praise you that our citizenship resides in heaven from which we eagerly await our Savior, Jesus Christ, who will transform our lowly bodies into the likeness of his glorious body (Phil 3:20-21). When Christ appears, we will be like him for we will see him as he is (1 Jn 3:2). I long for the day when I will see your face in righteousness and be satisfied with your likeness when I awake (Ps 17:15). For now, we see only a reflection as in a mirror, but then we will see face to face. Now we know in part, but then we will fully know (1 Cor 13:12). So, may I set my mind on things that are above, not on things that are on earth, for my life is protected in Christ (Col 3:2-3). Upon our deaths, we look forward to being received into your everlasting city, of which you are the architect and builder (Heb 11:10). In the meantime, help us to comfort and encourage one another (1 Thes 4:18; Heb 3:13). Now, may you and your beloved Son, who loved us and gave us eternal comfort and good hope through grace, comfort our hearts and establish us in every good work and word (2 Thes 2:16-17).

3.5.5. Additional good in life.

Lord, you told us godliness has value for all things, promising benefits in this life and the life to come (1 Tim 4:8); and that if we pursue your kingdom and your righteousness, you will give everything we need (Matt 6:33). And, you know everything we need (Matt 6:32), so I cast all my cares on you for you care for me (1 Pe 5:7).

3.5.6. Preservation from calamity.

You, Lord, are my refuge and my fortress, my God, in whom I trust. I find safety under your wings. Your faithfulness protects me like a shield. I don't need to fear terror by night or arrows that fly by day because you are my dwelling place and my refuge. No evil can conquer me (Ps 91:2-10). I'm so thankful you neither slumber nor sleep. You are my protector, and you stand at my right side as a protective shade. The sun cannot harm me by day nor the moon by night, for you keep my life from all evil. You protect me in all I do, now and forevermore (Ps 121:4-8).

3.5.7. Daily comfort and support.

O Sovereign God, extend your favor upon us. Please deliver us and grant us success (Ps 90:17, 118:25). May our sons and daughters flourish and reflect the beauty of your name. May our storehouses be full of every kind of provision. May our streets hear no cries of distress. We are blessed because you are our Lord (Ps 144:12-15), blessed in our cities, blessed in our fields, blessed when we come in, blessed when we go out (Dt 28:3-6), for all things work together for good to those who love you and are called according to your purpose (Rom 8:28). Now may Jesus Christ himself, who loved us and gave us eternal comfort and good hope through grace, comfort and establish our hearts in every good work and word (2 Thes 2:16-17).

3.5.8. God's promises fulfilled.

Father, because of your glory and excellence, you have given us great and precious promises (2 Pe 1:4) that have been fulfilled in Christ with a resounding "Yes" (2 Cor 1:20). So then, as your servant, may your promises be fulfilled to me (Lk 1:38; 2 Sm 7:25). May we joyously draw water from the springs of salvation (Is 12:3) and drink deeply and delight in your overflowing abundance (Is 66:11). Turn to me and show me your mercy, as you do for all who love your name (Ps 119:132). Do above and beyond all that we ask or think, according to your power at work within us (Eph 3:20) and your glorious riches in Christ Jesus (Phil 4:19).

4.
THANKSGIVINGS FOR MERCY

In our prayers we seek not only God's favor but also to give God the glory due his name by means of awe filled adoration of his infinite perfections and grateful acknowledgment of his goodness. Certainly, we add nothing to his glory, but he is pleased to accept it, assuming it comes from a heart that is humbly aware of its own unworthiness to receive any favor from God.

4.1. Abundant reasons for gratitude.

We are encouraged to praise God due the abundant reasons for which to be thankful. Lord, we thank you, along with your people throughout all time. We give thanks because your amazing deeds have revealed you are near (Ps 75:1). With all that is in us, we praise you. May we never forget the good things you have done for us (Ps 103:1-2). We praise you, for it is delightful and appropriate for us to sing your praises and declare your steadfast love in the morning and your faithfulness at night (Ps 147:1, 92:1-2). We praise you, our God and King. Every day we will praise you for your abundant goodness and righteousness (Ps 145:1-2, 7). We praise you, for you delight in your people. You crown the humble with victory. You honor the faithful. May your praises always be in our hearts and our mouths (Ps 149:1-6). As long as we live and have our being we will sing praises to you; and when we have no being on earth, we hope to have our being in heaven to be praising you all the better (Ps 146:2). Because of and through Jesus Christ, we offer a sacrifice of praise and thanksgiving to you, and with our lips proclaim our allegiance (Heb 13:15). In so doing, we offer a sacrifice that glorifies you and pleases you more than the sacrifice of an ox or bull (Ps 50:23, 69:31). We proclaim your unfailing love and praise you for all you have done. We rejoice in your goodness to your people, which was granted according to your mercy and love (Is 63:7).

4.2. Specificity in our thanksgiving.

We must be specific in our thanksgivings to God. We thank God for revealing to us, in his word, the goodness of his nature and many specific instances of his goodness. Father, we thank you as the God of gods for your steadfast love endures forever (Ps 136:1). On Mount Sinai, Moses desired to see your glory, and in a display of your compassion, you made all your goodness pass before him while declaring your name, Yahweh. (Ex 33:19). However, as a merciful and gracious God, you extend your goodness to all people, and your mercy is over all you have made. As one great chorus, your works and your saints offer you praise, speaking of the greatness of your kingdom and declaring your might (Ps 145:8-11). At times, we struggle to understand the affliction and suffering you permit, yet you do not enjoy bringing affliction and suffering. Even if you cause suffering, you will show compassion according to the abundance of your steadfast love (Lam 3:32-33). Lord, be pleased in our fear of you and our hope in your steadfast love (Ps 147:10).

4.3. Thankful for this present physical world. We are thankful for God's creatures and mankind in general.

We thank God for his providential care of the physical world and this present age. We thank God for his providential care with reference to all the creatures, and the world of mankind, in general. O Sovereign Creator, who laid the foundation of the earth resulting in the singing of the morning stars and joyful shouting of the sons of God. You command the morning and tell the dawn when to appear. You determine the territory and paths of light and darkness. You hold the keys to the storehouse of snow and hail and determine where light is distributed and wind is scattered. You crafted the channels for the rain and the path of the thunderbolt in order to satisfy the wasteland and make the ground sprout with grass. You command the clouds in order for a flood of waters to nourish the earth yet set a boundary that they cannot pass so as to not cover the earth. You empowered the lion to hunt its prey and the ravens to provide for their young. You determined for the wild donkey to run free and the wings of the ostrich to wave proudly. You gave the horse its might and allowed the hawk to spread its wings and soar (Jb 38-39; cf. Ps 104:5; Jer 31:35).

The highest heavens belong to you, but you have given the earth to mankind, given him dominion over your creation, and placed everything under his authority (Ps 115:16, 8:6; cf. Gn 9:2).

When I consider the heavens, the work of your hands, the moon and the stars; what is man that you are mindful of him? Of what importance is mankind that you should care? (Ps 8:3-4). You have covered yourself with light as if it were a robe and stretched out the heavens like a tent canopy (Ps 104:2). Why do you extend your grace to us?

Yet you give life and breath to every part of your creation (Acts 17:25). You cause the sun to rise on both the evil and the good and send rain on the righteous and the unrighteous (Matt 5:45). Even in past generations, as you allowed nations to go their own way, you did not leave them without evidence of you. You care for the earth and water it abundantly. You gave them rain from heaven and fruitful seasons. You satisfied them with food and brought joy to their hearts (Acts 14:17) You soften the earth with showers and bless its growth, soaking it furrows and leveling its ridges (Ps 65:9-10). You turn springs into streams that flow between the mountains and give drink to every beast of the field. The birds nest beside the streams and sing among the branches (Ps 104:10-12). You cause grass to grow for the cattle; and from the earth, you bring forth wine to gladden the heart of man, oil to make his face shine, and bread to provide him strength (Ps 104:14-15). Truly, every good and perfect gift comes from you, the Father of lights, who does not change like shifting shadows (Jam 1:17).

May your glory endure forever and may you rejoice in all your works (Ps 104:31). In the name of Christ who upholds the universe by the word of his power (Heb 1:3). Amen.

4.4. Thankful for mankind specifically.

We thank God for his particular care of mankind.

4.4.1. God gloriously created us with a glorious purpose.

Father Creator, while in the womb, amid our unformed substance, you intricately designed us, revealing your awesome and wonderful nature

(Ps 139:14-16). You designed us to be your image bearers and reflect your glory throughout your creation (Gn 1:27-28). You made us a little lower than yourself and crowned us with glory and honor (Ps 8:5).

You breathed into us the breath of life (Gn 2:7) and with your breath, the breath of the Almighty, you allow us to understand (Jb 32:8).

As believers, our bodies are the temple of the Holy Spirit who resides within us (1 Cor 6:19, 3:16). You purchased us with the great price of your own Son; therefore, we strive to glorify and honor you with our bodies (1 Cor 6:20). You formed us for yourself in order that we might declare your praise (Is 43:21).

4.4.2. God preserves our lives.

Jehovah Jireh, God our provider, with every bone in my body I will praise you. No one compares to you. Who else rescues the helpless from the strong? Who else protects the helpless and poor? (Ps 35:10). Each morning, I wake because you have sustained me (Ps 3:5, 4:8).

God, you should be praised; may the sound of praise from your people be heard. You have kept our souls among the living and have not allowed our feet to slip. Through fire, crushing burdens, and evil men, you have brought us to a place of abundance. So, we come to you in worship (Ps 66:8-13).

Jesus Christ, who is the radiance of your glory and the creator and sustainer of all created things (Heb 1:2-3), has promised to never leave us or forsake us (Heb 13:5). Additionally, you have sent out the angels, as ministering spirits, to serve those who will inherit salvation (Heb 1:14) and guard us in all our ways (Ps 91:11).

You alone are Lord. You made the heavens with all their hosts, the earth and all that is on it, the seas and all that is in them; and you preserve all of them. As a result, the host of heaven worships you (Neh 9:6). I add my voice to that great chorus of praise, for you will preserve me through every evil attack and bring me safely to your heavenly kingdom; to him be the glory forever and ever. Amen (2 Tim 4:18).

4.4.3. God protects amid sickness.

Jehovah Rophe, the snares of death encompass and lay hold on me. I suffer distress and anguish. Lord, deliver my soul! O righteous God, extend your grace and mercy to the simple and lowly. Deliver my soul from death, my eyes from tears, my feet from stumbling; and I will walk before you in the land of the living (Ps 116:3-9).

Grant that I would never despise your work but rather see you as the author of life and death (Jb 5:6; Ps 68:20). If it be your will give me good health (3 Jn 2). Comfort me (2 Cor 1:4). Secure my trust in you and steer me from self-reliance (Prv 3:5). Grant me endurance and encouragement amid suffering (Rom 15:4-6).

May I always look to Jesus and not grow weary or lose heart (Heb 12:1–3). Give me peace in Christ (Is 26:3), joy and faithfulness amid tribulation (Rom 12:12), and contentment in whatever circumstances you choose (Phil 4:11–13).

4.4.4. God provides support and comfort.

Lord, we thank you and praise you! You daily load us with benefits. You are the God of our salvation (Ps 68:19). You make us lie down in green pastures, lead beside still waters, and restore our souls. Even in the darkest valley you prepare a table in the presence of our enemies. You anoint our heads with oil, and our cup overflows (Ps 23:2-5).

We may serve you with little in our pockets or on our feet, but because of you we will lack nothing (Lk 22:35). You have watched over us; with a lamp shone over our heads and by your light we have walked through darkness (Jb 29:3).

May we never fix our hope on the uncertainty of riches but rather on you, who richly supplies us with all things to enjoy (1 Tim 6:17). In Christ, you have blessed us with every spiritual blessing in heavenly places (Eph 1:3). You, who called us to your marvelous glory and excellence, have given us everything we need to live a godly life by means of your rich knowledge (2 Pe 1:3). Therefore, we revel in your great goodness (Neh 9:25).

4.4.5. God generally provides success.

God, you arm me with strength and keep my way secure (Ps 18:32). Like Job, you place a wall of protection around me, and all my success flows from your provision (Jb 1:10). You even send angels to serve your people (Heb 1:14). I am unworthy of all the loving-kindness and faithfulness you have shown me (Gn 32:10). So then, our lives are full of joyful shouting for your salvation abides with us (Ps 118:15).

4.5. Thankful for God's redemptive plan.

4.5.1. God's redemptive plan for lost sinners.

Lord, we were foolish and disobedient, slaves to our various passions and desires. We thank you for revealing yourself as Savior in a display of your goodness and kindness. You saved us, not because of works we have done, but according to your mercy. You washed away our sins, giving us new birth and new life through the Holy Spirit (Tit 3:3-5).

No one ever cared for me, like you. No one else has shown me your compassion. I might as well have been thrown into the open field, despised on the day of my birth. Yet, you passed by my abandoned soul and said, "Live!" (Eze 16:5-6). You covered my nakedness and shame with your garment and declared me to be your own (Eze 16:8). When no one else could ransom my life because the cost was too high (Ps 49:7-8), you found a ransom who showed mercy and delivered me from going down into the pit (Jb 33:24).

We are all like water, spilled on the ground, with no means to be gathered again, but you devised a plan for the banished to be restored (2 Sm 14:14).

You chose not to spare the angels when they fell. You placed them in chains of utter darkness. You destroyed the ancient world, preserving only Noah, your herald of righteousness (2 Pe 2:4). Yet, while I was a sinner, you chose to demonstrate your love towards me by sending your Son to die for me (Rom 5:8; cf. Rom 5:6, 10; 1 Jn 4:9).

Therein lies the hidden wisdom you ordained before the ages for our glory. That which the eye could not see, the ear hear, or any mind imagine; you revealed to us through your Spirit (1 Cor 2:7-9). And for that, I will ever thank you!

4.5.2. God's eternal and divine election.

O Lord, God of our salvation (Ps 88:1), we praise you for day after day you bear us up (Ps 68:19). We praise you as our Rock. We exalt you as the God of our salvation (Ps 18:46). We must always praise and thank you as those you have loved and chose from the beginning for salvation through the sanctification by the Spirit and through belief in the truth (2 Thes 2:13).

You chose us in Christ before the foundation of the world to be holy and blameless in love before you. You predestined us to be adopted as sons through Jesus Christ, according to the good pleasure of your will and to the praise of your glorious grace (Eph 1:4-6).

We were yours, and you gave us to Christ (Jn 17:6), and in accordance with your will, Christ will lose none of all those you have given him, but raise them up at the last day (Jn 6:39).

4.5.3. God's appointment of a Redeemer.

Lord, I praise you as my redeemer. My redemption rests not in the blood of bulls and goats, for you find no pleasure in burnt offerings and sin offerings. However, when Christ came into the world, you prepared for him a body with which to come and do your will (Heb 10:4-7), and he delighted to do your will because your law was in his heart (Ps 40:8). Therefore, you delight in your chosen servant (Is 42:1). You are well pleased with the work of your Son (Matt 17:5).

So then, you have chosen to judge no one but have instead given all judgment to your Son, so that all people will honor the Son just as they honor you. The one who does not honor the Son does not honor you who sent him. You have life in yourself and have granted that same life-giving power and the authority to execute judgment to your Son. Therefore, whoever hears the Son's words and believes has eternal life and will not come into judgment (Jn 5:22-27, cf Jn 3:16, 35). Sin no longer rules over me, because I am not under law but under grace (Rom 6:14).

4.5.4. God's early revelation of his gracious design.

My sovereign Lord, we praise you for the immediate and gracious communication to fallen Adam and Eve of your plan to provide a Redeemer who would come through the offspring of woman to successfully crush the head of the serpent (Gn 3:15) – that ancient serpent, who is called the devil and Satan (Rv 12:9). However, your display of grace extends even further back for you had already determined to offer Jesus as the Lamb slain before the foundations of the world (Rv 13:8).

We praise you for the preservation of your promise in the salvation of Noah and his family (Gn 6:8); for the extension of your promise made to Abraham, that through him all the families of the earth would be blessed (Gn 12:3); and for the enhancement of your promise that through Judah, a king would come to whom belongs the obedience of every nation (Gn 49:10).

We praise you that by faith, you commended the saints of old, even though they did not receive what was promised (Heb 11:39). Yet, in some way, they rejoiced to see Christ's day (Jn 8:56).

4.5.5. God's favor to his people in the Old Testament.

O great deliverer, we marvel at your work of uprooting Israel out of Egypt like a grapevine; and driving out other nations in order to transplant them into your land (Ps 80:8-9). They won their land, not with their own sword or the might of their own arm. Rather, their salvation came from your right hand and your arm, and the light of your face, because you delighted in them (Ps 44:3).

What a blessing for the Jews to be entrusted with your spoken words (Rom 3:2), to be adopted as your children, the recipients of your glory, participants in your covenants, the beneficiaries of your law, the worshippers in your temple, and the heirs of your promises. Greater yet, to the Jews belong Christ, according to the flesh, who is God over all, blessed forever (Rom 9:4-5).

We praise you, for you have given rest to your people, according to all that you promised. Not one word has failed of all the good promises you gave through your servant Moses (1 Ki 8:56).

We marvel at the many times and varied ways you spoke through your prophets to your people of your coming grace (Heb 1:1; 1 Pe 1:10). We know they spoke, not of their own will, but were carried along by your Spirit (2 Pe 1:21). You revealed to them that they served not themselves but us, for these things have been announced to us through those who preach the gospel by the heaven-sent Holy Spirit — so amazing, even the angels long to look into these things (1 Pe 1:11-12).

Even though you approved them by their faith, they did not receive what you had promised, for you had determined to provide something better for us, and that apart from us they would not be made perfect (Heb 11:40). So, we praise and thank you as blessed recipients of your covenant promises.

4.6. Thankful for Christ's life and work.

4.6.1. Jesus Christ's incarnation.

Lord God, we thank you for the incarnation. When the appropriate time had come, you sent your son. In being born of woman, he took on our humanity, fulfilling the promise made to Eve (cf. Gn 3:15). He was born under the law in order to redeem those under the law, so that we might receive adoption as your sons (Gal 4:4-5).

We marvel at one of the great mysteries of our faith (1 Tim 3:16), that the eternal Word became flesh, and dwelt among us. We observed his glory — the glory of your one and only son — full of grace and truth (Jn 1:14). In fact, for this very purpose, Christ came into the world — to bear witness to the truth (Jn 18:37).

The Son of Man came to seek and to save the lost (Lk 19:10); so that we may have abundant life (Jn 10:10); so that he might destroy the works of the devil who has the power of death (1 Jn 3:8; Heb 2:14); so that he might save even the worst of sinners (1 Tim 1:15).

We thank you, for in taking on flesh and blood, Jesus Christ delivered us who were held in slavery all our lives to the fear of death. He was made like us in every respect, so that he might become a merciful and faithful high priest, to make atonement for our sins and bring many of your sons and daughters to glory (Heb 2:14-17, 11).

4.6.2. God's ongoing care of Christ during his incarnation.

Lord, we thank you for the encouragement of your ongoing care of your Son. Not only did you set apart Christ and send him into the world (Jn 10:36), but also set on him your seal of approval and never left him alone, for he always does what pleases you (Jn 6:27, 8:29).

We praise you, for in Christ, you reconciled the world to yourself, not counting our trespasses against us (2 Cor 5:19), bringing peace, good will, and life through him (Lu 2:14; 1 Jn 4:9).

Thank you for giving him authority over everyone, so that he can give eternal life to all you have given him (Jn 17:2).

4.6.3. Jesus Christ's perfect and exemplary teaching and life.

I glorify you the God of Israel (Matt 15:31) for the varied ways you communicated to your people throughout the Old Testament. However, in these days, you have spoken more clearly to us through your Son (He 1:1-2). His teachings are not his own but rather yours (Jn 7:16) and possess an authority unlike anyone else (Matt 7:29)

Lord, I often reflect Nicodemus' uncertainty but am also left with his conclusion. No logic suffices other than, Jesus was a teacher sent by God – how else could he have performed the miracles he did (Jn 3:2). His very works bear witness that you sent him (Jn 5:36). The blind receive their sight, lepers are cleansed, the deaf hear, the dead are raised, and the poor have the gospel preached to them (Matt 11:5). Even the winds and sea obey him (Matt 8:27). Truly, he is the Son of God (Matt 27:54).

In coming, Christ also left an example for us to follow. He never sinned and no deceit was found in his mouth. He did not retaliate when he was insulted, nor threaten revenge when he suffered. Instead, he trusted you to appropriately judge (1 Pe 2:21-23). This is the kind of high priest we need: holy, innocent, undefiled, separated from sinners, and exalted above the heavens (Heb 7:26).

So then, since Christ suffered in this way, we should arm ourselves with the same attitude (1 Pe 4:1). We say we abide in him, so we should walk just as he walked (1 Jn 2:6). In following his example, you perfect love in us, and we can face you with confidence because we live like Jesus here in the world (1 Jn 4:17).

4.6.4. His call to poor sinners.

Lord, may I, like John the Baptist, rejoice as I look on Jesus Christ, the Lamb of God, who takes away the sin of the world (Jn 1:29). You gave him all authority on earth to forgive (Matt 9:6), so he came to save his people from their sins (Matt 1:21). He came, not to call the righteous, but rather befriended the tax collectors and sinners, calling them to repentance (Matt 11:19, 9:13).

I am so thankful for Jesus' gracious invitation to those who are weary and heavy laden, to come and receive rest (Matt 11:28); to those who are thirsty, to come and drink (Jn 7:37). And more importantly, he will never cast out all those who come (Jn 6:37).

4.6.5. Complete satisfaction for sin and resulting privileges.

Great God of wonders, we thank you for your strange and matchless grace manifest in miraculous love. While we were still sinners, Christ died for us; while we were enemies you reconciled us to yourself through the death of your Son (Rom 5:8, 10). This is love: not that we loved you, but that you loved us and sent your Son to be our atoning sacrifice for sins (1 Jn 4:10) and not ours only but the sins of the whole world (1 Jn 2:2).

Your Son, Jesus Christ, tasted death for everyone so that through his death, he might destroy the devil who holds the power of death (Heb

2:9, 14) and disarm and disgrace rulers and authorities having triumphed over them by the cross (Col 2:14-15).

We thank you and marvel that by one single offering, Christ has perfected for all time those who are being sanctified (Heb 10:14); that he has put an end to rebellion, brought sin to completion, atoned for iniquity, and ushered in perpetual righteousness (Dn 9:24).

He has redeemed us from the curse of the law by becoming a curse for us (Gal 3:13). He condemned sin in the flesh by becoming like sinful flesh (Rom 8:3). He appeared once, at the end of the ages, to put away sin by the sacrifice of himself (Heb 9:26), entered the Most Holy Place once for all time and secured our redemption forever (Heb 9:12).

He was pierced for our transgressions, crushed for our iniquities. The punishment for our peace was on him, and we are healed by his wounds. By your will, you laid on him all our iniquity, crushing him and putting him to grief (Is 53:5, 6, 10).

My broken soul finds rest for Jesus is my peace. Being far from you, without hope, he brought me near (Eph 2:12-14), freed us from our sins, and made us a kingdom of priests for your glory (Rv 1:5-6).

Worthy is the Lamb who was slain, to receive power and wealth and wisdom and might and honor and glory and blessing; for you were slain and have redeemed us to God by Your blood out of every tribe and tongue and people and nation (Rv 5:12, 9).

4.6.6. His resurrection from the dead.

Lord, we thank you that even though Jesus was delivered over because of our sins, you raised him to life for the sake of our justification (Rom

4:25) and declared him to be the powerful Son of God (Rom 1:4). You raised him, releasing him from the pains of death and corruption, making him both Lord and Christ. You raised him because it was not possible for him to be held in death's power (Acts 2:24, 31, 36).

He now lives forever and holds the keys of death and Hades (Rv 1:18). Death no longer has dominion over him (Rom 6:9).

Gloriously, Jesus serves as the first resurrection to eternal life and offers a pledge and proof of the resurrection of his people. We all died in Adam, but in Christ are made alive (1 Cor 15:20-23).

Christ died and rose again for this very reason — to be Lord both of the living and the dead (Rom 14:9), so whether we are awake or asleep, we will live together with him (1 Thes 5:10).

4.6.7. His ascension and position at God's right hand.

To the one who sits enthroned on high (Ps 113:5), we thank you for raising our Lord Jesus and seating him at your right hand (Mk 16:19). We have this hope as an anchor for our soul, safe and secure. Christ has entered the inner sanctuary behind the curtain, into heaven itself, appearing before you on our behalf as our high priest and forerunner (Heb 6:19-20, 9:24).

Seated at your right hand on the throne of Majesty in heaven (Heb 8:1), angels, authorities, and all powers have been subjected to him (1 Pe 3:22).

In your home there is more than enough room in which he prepares for us a place (Jn 14:2). Even though we cannot follow him now, my heart is not troubled, for we will follow him later (Jn 13:36). He will come again to receive us to himself, so that where he is there we will also be (Jn 14:3).

4.6.8. His ongoing intercession for his redeemed.

Jesus Christ, our great High Priest, we praise and thank you for bearing the sins of many and interceding for rebels (Is 53:12). We are thankful that your intercession extends beyond your disciples to all those who believe in you through their message (Jn 17:20).

In our sin, we come to the Father through you because you serve as our righteous advocate and constant intercessor, through whom we gain access to the Father and complete salvation (1 Jn 2:1, Heb 7:25)

We will hold fast to our confession because, in you, we have a great High Priest who has passed into the heavens, behind the veil. We have a great High Priest who can sympathize with our weaknesses, who was tempted as we are, yet without sin. So, we draw near to our Father with confidence, expecting to receive grace and mercy in our time of need (Heb 4:14-16).

4.6.9. His exalted position as Sovereign Redeemer.

Most High God, we thank you for exalting Jesus Christ after he humbled himself and became obedient to the point of death, even death on a cross. You gave him a name that is above every name, that at the name of Jesus every knee will bow and every tongue confess that Jesus Christ is Lord, to your great glory (Phil 2:8-11).

You gave him all authority in heaven and on earth (Matt 28:18). You have crowned him with glory and honor putting everything in subjection under his feet (Heb 2:7-9).

You have declared him to be King of kings and Lord of lords (Rv 19:16). You, the Ancient of Days, have given him dominion and glory and a kingdom, an everlasting dominion and a kingdom that will not be destroyed (Dn 7:13-14).

The government will forever rests on his shoulders, and his name is Wonderful Counselor, Mighty God, Eternal Father, Prince of Peace. There will be no end to his peace and the increase of his government. He will establish justice and righteousness forevermore (Is 9:6-7).

You have placed your king on Zion, your holy hill (Ps 2:6), and he will reign over the house of Jacob forever (Lk 1:33) until he has destroyed all dominion, authority, and power, until he puts all enemies under his feet (1 Cor 15:24-25; Eph 6:12; Heb 10:13). He will then turn the kingdom over to you, so that you may be all in all (1 Cor 15:24, 28).

4.6.10. Certainty of his second coming.

We praise you, our Just and Sovereign God, who has set a day when Jesus Christ, who you raised from the dead, will justly judge the world (Acts 17:31).

Our Lord Jesus will appear from Heaven, coming with his mighty angels. They will gather out of his kingdom everything that causes sin and all who do evil. In flaming fire, He will bring judgment on those who do not know God and do not obey the gospel of our Lord Jesus.

But also, on that day, he will send out his angels to gather his elect from one end of the heavens to the other. He will come to be glorified in his saints and admired by all who believed (2 Thes 1:7-10; Matt 13:41; Matt 24:31). On that day, the righteous will shine like the sun in their Father's kingdom (Matt 13:43).

So, we wait for new heavens and a new earth in which God's righteousness dwells. Lord, while we wait, strengthen us in making every effort to be found spotless, blameless, and at peace with him (2 Pe 3:13-14). And then, Lord Jesus, come quickly (Rv 22:20).

4.7. Thankful for God's Word and Christ's Church.

4.7.1. Sending of the Holy Spirit into the believer.

We thank you for displaying your goodness and loving-kindness through the regenerating and renewing work of the Holy Spirit, whom you poured out richly on us through Jesus Christ (Tit 3:3-7). We find great comfort and gratitude in that he seals us with his promise, guaranteeing our inheritance until we acquire possession of it (Eph 1:13-14; cf. 1 Pe 1:3-5). Gloriously, you have promised to complete the work you started in each of us through the work of the Holy Spirit (Phil 1:6).

Not only did the Spirit regenerate our sinful hearts, but he continues the work of sanctifying our new hearts. Through his work, we are being transformed into the image of our Lord, one degree of glory to another (2 Cor 3:18). He fills us (Eph 5:18) in order to obey (Eze 36:26-27). He keeps us from gratifying the desires of our flesh (Gal 5:16). He convicts us of our sin (Jn 16:8). He produces love, joy, peace, patience, kindness, goodness, faithfulness, gentleness, self-control (Gal 5:22-23). He guides us into all truth and reveals Jesus (Jn 15:26, 16:13-15).

Through the Spirit, we are adopted into your family and call you Father (Rom 8:16-17). And within this family, he distributes spiritual gifts to each of us as he so desires (1 Cor 12:11) for the general encouragement and care of the whole body of Christ (1 Cor 12).

Thank you Father for the comprehensive work of the Spirit and that he will sustain us to the end, guiltless in the day of our Lord Jesus Christ (1 Cor 1:8).

4.7.2. Covenant of grace and its precious privileges.

We are thankful that in Jesus Christ you made an everlasting covenant with us, and though the mountains may depart, and the hills be removed, this covenant of your peace will never be removed (Is 54:10). By means of your divine power and Christ's mediation, you have given us great and precious and better promises, and through these promises we are enabled to share in the divine nature (2 Pe 1:4; Heb 8:6).

Even though, as a loving Father, you punish us, you will never remove your steadfast love nor allow your faithfulness to fail (Ps 89:32-33).

You desire for the heirs of your promise to be certain of your unchangeable character, so you bound yourself with an oath, and we know it is impossible for you to lie. Therefore, we flee to you for refuge and hold fast to the hope set before us (Heb 6:17-18).

In the name of Jesus Christ and because of his new covenant work, we come to you. Amen.

4.7.3. Inspiration and preservation of Scripture.

Our great revealing God, we thank you for the Scriptures, and that in searching them, we may have eternal life because they bear witness of Jesus Christ (Jn 5:39). Thank you for gifting your divinely inspired Word which is profitable for teaching, reproof, correction, and training in righteousness (2 Tim 3:16). Your Scriptures were written long ago for our instruction and so we may have hope (Rom 15:4). Therefore, we would do well to pay close attention to them as to a lamp shining in a dark place (2 Pe 1:19).

We praise you that the words of your Scriptures are not sealed (Is 29:11) but that, in our own tongue, we hear of the mighty works of God (Acts 2:11).

We thank you, Father, Lord of heaven and earth, that those things which were hidden from the wise and understanding, to many prophets and kings, you have revealed to us children, and you were pleased to do it this way (Lk 10:21, 24).

4.7.4. Institution of the ordinances.

Lord, we thank you for instituting the divine ordinances which consists of both an outward, visible sign and an inward, spiritual grace. You have ordained bread and wine, which is our visible food, to picture to our minds the food of our souls (Jn 6:53-57). You have ordained water, by which we visibly wash, to convey our spiritual cleansing through Christ's death, burial, and resurrection.

We thank you as we consider the institution of the Lord's Supper by Jesus himself. It was the Lord, who on the night he was betrayed, took the bread and then the cup, and having blessed them, gave them to his disciples (Mk 14:22-25; Matt 26:26-29). May your divinity be stamped on this meal. May we approach with holy awe and reverence. Create in us a heavenly mindset, when we celebrate so heavenly an institution. And may we reflect the unity within our church. We who are many are one body, for we all partake of the one bread (1 Cor 10:17).

We thank you that all of us who have been baptized in Christ Jesus have been baptized into his death, so that as Christ was raised from the dead through the glory of the Father, now we also may live new lives (Rom 6:3-4; Col 2:12).

4.7.5. Institution and expansion of the church.

We thank you for making powerful the preaching of Jesus Christ according to your eternal command and the gospel now revealed to all nations, bringing about the obedience of faith. Through them strongholds have been torn down (Rom 16:25-26; 2 Cor 10:4), and the body of Christ, the church, has multiplied.

Even though your people boldly proclaimed amid great conflict (1 Thes 2:2), the gospel continued to increase and mightily prevail (Acts 19:20), turning many away from idols to serve the living and true God and wait for his Son from heaven (1 Thes 1:9-10).

We rejoice as people continue to come to faith in Christ Jesus and display their transformation through their love of the saints. They possess a new hope laid up for them in heaven. This gospel has come to the whole world and is bearing fruit and increasing (Col 1:3-6).

God, we observe your powerful hand, and with the ancient King Darius, proclaim, "You are the living God and enduring forever. Your kingdom will not be destroyed, and your dominion will never end (Dn 6:26).

Then, in the fullness of time, you revealed to Mary that Jesus would come and be the Son of the Most High. He will reign over the house of Jacob forever, and his kingdom will never end (Lu 1:33). He will reign on the throne of David and over his kingdom, establishing and upholding it with justice and righteousness forever (Is 9:7).

We praise you, for in being part of your church, we also dwell within your kingdom. As Jesus declared to Peter, "on this rock I will build my church, and the gates of hell shall not prevail against it" (Matt 16:18). With Christ, we have been established forever, along with his throne as long as heaven lasts (Ps 89:29).

We thank you for our future hope of dwelling in your eternal kingdom, where there will no longer be any night, no need of a lamp or the light of the sun, because you will give us light and will reign forever and ever (Rv 22:5).

4.7.6. Godly examples throughout church history.

Our Heavenly Father, we thank you for so many who have faithfully served you through great endurance, in persecutions, in difficulties, in distresses (2 Cor 6:4); who have been delivered up to synagogues and prisons, brought before kings and governors for Christ's sake (Lu 21:12). They used these moments to testify of you, and you gave them wisdom no adversary could resist or refute (Lu 21:13-15).

For Christ's sake, they faced death all day long and were counted as sheep to be slaughtered. Despite all these things, they were more than victorious through him who loved us (Rom 8:36-37).

And ultimately, we praise you for the salvation and the kingdom that is to come with Christ, for he has overcome and thrown down the accuser of our brothers, and they triumphed over him by the blood of the Lamb and by the word of their testimony. They did not love their lives so much as to shrink from death (Rv 12:10-11).

We thank you for the great cloud of witnesses surrounding us, encouraging us (Heb 12:1), for the many examples among us who model a godly walk (Phil 3:17), for our spiritual ancestors who were commended for their faith and patiently wait for the promises (Heb 11:2, 6:12). Lord, help us to follow them as they followed Christ (1 Cor 11:1).

4.7.7. Spiritual communion of saints throughout time.

Our loving Father, we thank you that as we walk in the light, we have fellowship with one another (1 Jn 1:7), with all those sanctified saints, in every place who call on the name of Jesus Christ our Lord – both their Lord and ours (1 Cor 1:2).

We who are many are one body (2 Cor 10:17), possessing different gifts but the same Spirit, different kinds of service but the same Lord, varieties of activities but the same God empowering them all in everyone (1 Cor 12:4-6).

Thank you for uniting all your children who are scattered around the world (Jn 11:52), through Christ, who is the head of the body, the church (Col 1:18). You have graciously provided us with brothers and partners in suffering and in God's Kingdom and in the patient endurance to which Jesus calls us (Re 1:9).

4.7.8. Prospect and hope of eternal life.

Father, we thank you for the crown of life which you have promised to those who love you (Ja 1:12) and an inheritance that is imperishable, undefiled, and unfading, kept in heaven for us (1 Pe 1:4).

Here, we have no lasting city, but rather seek the city that is to come (Heb 13:14). We seek a better country, a heavenly one, with a firm foundation having you as its architect and builder (Heb 11:16, 10).

We, to whom you have extended your grace, place our hope in and know with certainty that we possess the eternal life you have promised, and we know you cannot lie (Ti 1:2; 1 Jn 5:13).

4.8. Thankful for spiritual mercies to those effectually called.

4.8.1. The Holy Spirit's work and our consciences.

Our Father and Redeemer, thank you for not abandoning us to our debased and worthless minds (Rom 1:28), for not allowing us to become hypocritical liars, seared in consciences (1 Ti 4:2), for not leaving us alone due an attachment to idols (Hos 4:17).

Instead, you have poured out your Spirit on us (Is 44:3), giving us life both physically and spiritually (Jb 34:14-15; Jn 3:6-7), empowering us for service and spiritual battle (Ac 1:8; Matt 12:28), cleansing, purifying, and sanctifying us (1 Cor 6:11), revealing and enlightening your Word (2 Pe 1:21; 1 Cor 2:12), providing a guarantee of our heavenly future (2 Cor 1:22), guiding and directing us daily (Rom 8:14; Gal 5:16), and producing unity and fellowship within your people (Ac 2:44-47).

4.8.2. Our Spirit led, transformed lives.

God, our great Creator, you have commanded the morning, and caused the dawn to know its place (Jb 38:12-13). In Jesus Christ, the sunrise has visited us from on high, bringing salvation (Lk 1:77-78). May the Sun of righteousness arise upon my soul with healing in his wings (Mal 4:2) and my path be as the light of dawn (Prv 4:18). I praise you for delivering us from the domain of darkness and transferring us to the kingdom of your beloved Son (Col 1:13) with whom we are now called into fellowship (1 Cor 1:9). We used to be far away from you, but you have brought us near and united us with Christ through his blood (Eph 2:13).

We thank you for all those to whom the gospel has come, not only in word, but in power as the Holy Spirit brought full assurance (1 Thes 1:2, 5).

Thank you for loving us with an everlasting love and continuing to extend faithful love to us (Jer 31:3), leading us with cords of kindness and bands of love (Hos 11:4).

4.8.3. Our forgiveness and peace of mind.

O gracious God, we praise you for our redemption through Christ's blood, the forgiveness of our sins, in accordance with the riches of your grace, with which you have lavished upon us in wisdom and understanding (Eph 1:7-8).

You forgive all our iniquities and heal all our diseases (Ps 103:3). In love you have delivered our lives from the pit of destruction and cast all our sins behind your back (Is 38:17).

Thank you for declaring us righteous by faith and bringing us peace with yourself through Jesus Christ. Through him we have access to you. We now rejoice in the hope of your glory (Rom 5:1-2).

4.8.4. Our sanctification, preservation, and strength.

Heavenly Father, you will not break a bruised reed or snuff out a smoldering wick (Matt 12:20) or despise the day of small things (Zec 4:10), but I continue to stand to this day because of your help (Ac 26:22). When I cry out to you, you answer me, make me bold, and strengthen my soul (Ps 138:3).

So often I am foolish and ignorant. My feet have come close to stumbling. My steps have almost slipped. But you are always with me, holding me up by my right hand, guiding me with your counsel, and will receive me to glory (Ps 73:22-24, 2).

If your law had not been my delight, I would have died in misery, so I will never forget your precepts, for by them you have preserved my life (Ps 119:92-93). If you had not been my help, my soul would have laid down in the silence of death. Lord, when I thought my foot had slipped, your loving kindness held me up. When my anxious thoughts overwhelm me, your comfort delights my soul (Ps 94:17-19).

4.8.5. Personal communion and favor with God.

Thank you for your gracious gift of faith in Christ, for through that faith I find pleasure with you (Heb 11:6). In Christ, you have blessed us and protected us, shined upon us and been gracious to us, looked on us with favor and given us peace (Num 6:24-26).

You have brought us to your holy mountain and have made us joyful in your house of prayer (Is 56:7, cf Heb 12:22 ff.). How good it is to draw near to you, for you are our refuge. We will declare all the wonderful things you have done (Ps 73:28).

A day in your courts is better than a thousand anywhere else. I would rather be at the door of your house than live in the tents of wicked people. You are my sun and shield. You give grace and glory and withhold no good thing from those who live with integrity. O Lord of hosts, blessed is the one who trusts in you (Ps 84:10-12).

4.8.6. Gracious answers to our prayers.

Lord, we have reason to love you because you have heard our voice and our prayers for mercy. Out of the depths we cry to you, and you have inclined your ear unto us, so we will call out to you as long as we live (Ps 116:1-2, 130:1).

Not only that, before we call you answer, and while we are yet speaking you hear us (Is 65:24). You answer, "Here I am," and you draw near to us whenever we call to you (Is 58:9; Dt 4:7). You hear the desire of the afflicted and strengthen their heart (Ps 10:17).

Praise be to God, who has not rejected our prayers or withheld his love from us (Ps 66:20).

4.8.7. Support amid and spiritual value of affliction.

Praise be to the Lord, for you have shown me the wonders of your steadfast love (Ps 31:21). You have seen my affliction and known the distress of my soul (Ps 31:7) and have comforted me in all my affliction. I share in Christ's sufferings, but you also shower me with your comfort in Christ (2 Cor 1:4-5).

No affliction seems pleasant at the time, but painful. Later on, however, it produces the fruit of peace and righteousness, for our benefit, so that we may share in your holiness (Heb 12:11,10). It is good for me to be afflicted so that I can learn your statutes. Before I was afflicted I went astray, but now I keep your word (Ps 119:71, 67).

In this I rejoice, even though I endure trials for a little while, these trials will show my faith to be genuine. I pray that the trials of my faith will bring you much praise and honor and glory when Jesus returns. We love and trust him even though we have never seen him. Even though we do not see him, we rejoice with a joy unspeakable and glorious, longing to receive the goal of our faith, the salvation of our souls (1 Pe 1:6-9).

4.8.8. God's promises fulfilled.

Lord, you are good to your servant, just as you promised (Ps 119:65). You always remember your covenantal decrees, the promises you made to a thousand generations (Ps 105:8). Not one word has failed of all the wonderful promises you have made to your people (1 Ki 8:56).

How could I repay you for all your acts of kindness to me? My soul will again rest in you, for you have been good to me. I will lift up my cup of salvation and praise you for saving me (Ps 116:12, 7). You are good. Your lovingkindness endures forever, and you are faithful to every generation (Ps 100:5). I will praise you at all times. As long as I live, praise will continually be in my mouth (Ps 34:1, 104:33). I hope to soon praise you with the living creatures who never rest day or night saying, "Holy, holy, holy, Lord God Almighty (Rv 4:8).

5.
INTERCESSION FOR OTHERS

Jesus taught us to pray with and for others, and Paul exhorted us to stay alert with intercession for all the saints (Eph 6:18). Additionally, throughout many of his prayers Paul prays for his friends. As we approach this trim element of prayer, let us not become indifferent because we are not particularly concerned with it, but rather let a holy fire of love for God and man, make our intercession warm and lively.

5.1. The lost.

5.1.1. The lost in general.

Lord, we know you are pleased when we pray for all people, for you desire all people to be saved and understand the truth of Jesus Christ who gave himself as a ransom for many (1 Tim 2:1-6).Look with compassion upon a world lying under the control of the evil one (1 Jn 5:19). Cast out the prince of this world (Jn 12:31), who has blinded the minds of unbelievers, keeping them from seeing the light of Christ's glorious gospel (2 Cor 4:4).

Be gracious to us. Make your face shine on us so that your way may be known on earth, your steadfast love and faithfulness, your saving power and righteousness among all the nations. Let all the peoples praise you, O God. Let the nations be glad and sing for joy for you judge fairly and govern with justice. May the ends of the earth see your salvation (Ps 67:1-4, 98:2-3).

May all the kingdoms of this world become the kingdom of our Lord and of his Christ who will reign forever and ever (Re 11:15).

5.1.2. Spread of gospel and growth of church

Lord, motivated by your love and empowered by your sovereignty, may your gospel be preached in all the world to every creature (Mk 16:15), for how can they call on him they have not believed in? How can they believe in the one whom they have not heard? How can they hear without someone preaching to them? And how are they to preach unless you send them? (Rom 10:14-15). Therefore, we pray to you, the Lord of the harvest, to send out workers into your harvest (Matt 9:38). Shine a great light on all those living in darkness, on those who dwell in the region and shadow of death (Matt 4:16).

Add to your church daily those being saved (Ac 2:47). Gather your people from the east and west. Say to the north, give up, and to the south, do not hold back. Bring your sons from far away, and your daughters from the ends of the earth; everyone who belongs to you, whom you created and formed for your glory (Is 43:5-7). May the earth be filled with the knowledge of Christ, just as the waters completely fill the sea (Is 11:9).

5.1.3. The conversion of the Jews.

Lord, while we thank you for allowing us Gentiles, a wild offshoot, to be grafted into the people of God, we grieve the unbelief that broke off the branches of Israel. We pray those broken branches may be grafted in again to your people. Even though they have continued in unbelief, let the fullness of the Gentiles come to Christ, and let all Israel be saved (Rom 11:17, 23-26). Pour out your grace and mercy on Israel, so they look on him whom they have pierced and turn to you (Zec 2:10). Let the veil which covers their hearts be removed as they come to the Lord (2 Cor 3:15-16).

5.1.4. Conversion of those who have rejected the Gospel.

Father of mercies, send your Spirit to convict and draw unbelievers to yourself (Jn 16:8; Eze 36:27). Remove their heart of stone and give them a new heart (Eze 11:19). Open their eyes to see the truth, so they will repent and call on the name of the Lord and be saved (Acts 3:19; Rom 10:13; 2 Tim 2:25–26). May those who have gone astray, return to the Shepherd and Overseer of their souls (1 Pe 2:25).

Bring believers into their lives who will live out and verbally share the gospel with them (Rom 10:14). May those who will not be won by the word be won by the behavior of Christians (1 Pe 3:1).

5.2. God's People.

5.2.1. The church in general.

Triune God, produce unity amid diversity within your church like the unity we will eternally experience (Rom 12:5; Jn 17:20-23; Eph 4:3; Rv 7:9). Form a church community that expects and exhibits discipleship as an ordinary part of the Christian life (2 Tim 2:2; 1 Thes 2:8).

Keep our elders and leadership above reproach and fit for ministry (1 Tim 3:1; Titus 1:6). Prepare faithful elders to use Scripture to equip members to do the work of ministry, resulting in the discipleship of all ages throughout the church (2 Tim 4:2; Eph 4:12; 2 Tim 2:2).

Give our church a hunger for scriptural truth (2 Tim 3:14–16) and preaching that is both Biblical and Spirit empowered (Acts 6:4; Heb 3:7). Produce in us meaningful transparent relationships. Allow isolation and anonymity to become abnormal (Acts 2:44–45; Eph 4:15–16). Help us grow in prayer (Phil 4:6; Lk 18:1; Jer 33:3).

Empower us and give us a desire to be distinct from the world (Rom 12:1–2; cf. Eph 4:17, 1 Jn 2:15-17). Help us give with joy as we give faithfully and sacrificially (2 Cor 9:7).

Embolden us to share the gospel and see more conversions. Prompt more members to consider their careers as an avenue to take the gospel to new places (Acts 1:8; cf. Matt 28:19-20). Prepare us for persecution (2 Tim 3:12). Help us find hope in heaven and not in earthly politics (Rom 13:1; 2 Pe 3:13).

Grace be with all who have undying love for our Lord Jesus Christ (Eph 6:24)

5.2.2. Spirit's outpouring to mend and revive the Church.

Lord, we thank you for the transforming work of the Holy Spirit in people's lives and the resulting evidence of their sincere faith in Jesus Christ and their love for others (Col 1:3-4). We are thankful for the expansion of the gospel and how it bears fruit and increases (Col 1:6). However, in a world which seems to become more and more corrupt, we long for the Holy Spirit to work both within the church and our lost world. May our sufferings produce endurance, character, and hope as your love is poured into our hearts through the Holy Spirit whom you have given (Rom 5:3-5). May your church be filled with the knowledge of your will in all spiritual wisdom and understanding, so as to walk in a worthy manner, fully pleasing to you; bearing fruit in every good work and increasing in a knowledge of you. May your church be strengthened with all power, according to your glorious might, for all endurance and patience with joy (Col 1:9-11).

Produce within the church a pure religion that is undefiled before you (Ja 1:27), a kingdom, which is not eating and drinking but righteousness and peace and joy in the Holy Spirit (Rom 14:17). Lord, I am filled with awe by your amazing works. In this time of our deep need, help us again as you did in years gone by. And in your anger, remember mercy (Hab 3:2).

5.2.3. Defeat of the church's enemies.

Our Sovereign and Almighty God, we praise you, for in Christ's death and resurrection, he has already defeated our enemies. Through his resurrection, he has gone into heaven and is at your right hand, with angels, authorities, and powers having been subjected to him (1 Pe 3:21-22).

However, for a time, until his return, we continue to fight a spiritual battle. So then, like Hezekiah, we pray. O Lord of hosts, God of Israel, you are enthroned between the mighty cherubim! You alone are God of all the kingdoms of the earth. You alone created the heavens and the earth. Bend down, O Lord, and listen! Open your eyes, O Lord, and see! Listen to our world's words of defiance against you. It is true, Lord, the leaders of this world have led the nations into corruption and destruction. They worship gods of immorality, greed, and power. Now, O Lord our God, rescue us from this world's power; then all the kingdoms of the earth will know that you alone, O Lord, are God (Is 37:15-20).

We sing with the elders of Christ, "You are worthy for you were slain, and with your blood you purchased for God people from every tribe and language and people and nation" (Re 5:9). May the gospel of your kingdom be proclaimed throughout the world as a testimony to all nations (Matt 24:14), until all the ends of the earth remember and turn to you, and all the families of the nations worship before you (Ps 22:27-28).

5.2.4. Suffering churches and persecuted believers.

Jehovah Shammah, remember those who suffer for Christ. Be present and protect them according to your will (Matt 26:39). Send them relief from heaven above. Deliver your saints from hateful enemies too strong for them (Heb 13:3; Ps 18:16–19). Preserve the righteous from being tempted to respond in sinful ways to their mistreatment (Lk 6:27–31). Strengthen the patience and faith of your suffering saints (Rv 13:10; Lam 3:26). Give them boldness to speak your truth with the right words in the right timing (Eph 6:19–20). Grace them with an understanding and experience of your peace amid their weakness. Give them hope (2 Cor 12:9). Draw them to you for their power (2 Cor 1:7–9). Hear their prayers (Ps 79:11). Open the eyes and soften the hearts of those who are persecuting (Matt 5:44; Eze 18:23).

We remember those who are suffering, as though we were suffering with them, since we are all in the body (Heb 13:3). Let the groans of the prisoners come before you; according to your great power, preserve those doomed to die (Ps 79:11). In this moment, we cry out for the endurance and faith of the saints (Rv 13:10). Hear our cries.

5.3. God's sovereignty over nations.

5.3.1. Nations of the world.

Our Father and King of all, dominion belongs to you, and you rule over the nations (Ps 22:28). Appropriately, all should fear you as the King of the nations. Among all the wise leaders of nations and in all their kingdoms there is none like you (Jer 10:6). You maintain justice, sitting enthroned as the righteous judge, ruling the people with fairness (Ps 9:4, 8).

So then Lord, quickly bring in the time in which you will make wars cease to the ends of the earth; when you break the bow and shatter the spear; when you burn the shields with fire (Ps 46:9); when you hammer swords into plowshares and spears into pruning hooks; when nations will never again train for war (Is 2:4).

We long for and pray for the day when you, the God of heaven, will set up a kingdom that will never be destroyed. May your plans stand firm forever and the intentions of your heart never be shaken (Ps 33:11).

5.3.2. National mercies.

King of the nations, hear our plea, and listen to our cries. Bring salvation to the people of this nation. Fix our brokenness. Manifest your glory through our redemption.

We grieve Satan's work of blinding our nation, keeping unbelievers from seeing the light of the gospel of the glory of Christ (2 Cor 4:4). We ask you to do a spiritual work in our nation. Without your grace, we will be destroyed. Listen to the cries of believers in this nation. Open your eyes to our inevitable destruction. We do not come to you based on our righteous acts but based on your abundant compassion (Dn 9:16-18). May we repent and turn to Christ, receiving forgiveness of sin (1 Jn 1:9) and producing a righteousness that exalts a nation, for sin is a reproach to any people (Prv 14:34).

Lord, show us your unfailing love and grant us your salvation. Produce in this nation a fear of you. Let truth spring from the earth and righteousness smile down from heaven. Pour out your blessings (Ps 85:7, 9). We come with expectation, because your lovingkindness never ceases, and your compassion never fails (Lam 3:22).

In your sovereignty, you placed us here in this time (Acts 17:26). May we submit to our governing authorities, for there is no authority except for those you have established (Rom 13:1). We ask you to divinely work in our governing authorities, so we may live peaceful and quiet lives in all godliness and holiness (1 Tim 2:1-2; Jer 29:7; 1 Pe 2:17).

Since the heart of every leader flows through your hand like a stream, direct our leaders to love you and submit to your rule in their lives (Ps 21:1; Prv 11:14). You make nations great, and you destroy them. You enlarge nations, and you disperse them. Therefore, give our leaders reason, so we don't wander in a trackless wasteland (Jb 12:23-24).

5.3.3. Advancement of the Gospel in our nation.

Jesus, Great Light of the World, we ask you to not remove the spiritual influence of churches spread throughout our nation, even though we deserve it because we have left our first love (Rv 2:4-5).

May we never experience a famine in our nation – a famine from hearing your words. May we never be forced to wander from sea to sea, and from north to south, searching for the words of the Lord, only to never find them (Amos 8:11-12).

Let wisdom, knowledge, and the abundance of salvation be the stability of our times (Is 33:6). Let the righteous flourish and peace abound, till the moon be no more, and may there be those who fear you as long as the sun and moon endure, throughout all generations (Ps 72:5, 7). May following generations, a people yet to be created, come to praise you (Ps 102:18).

5.3.4. Political leaders.

O Sovereign God, who presides over heaven's court and pronounces judgment on heavenly beings (Ps 82:1), give wisdom and understanding to our leaders, a spirit of knowledge and a fear of you (Ps 105:22). May they lead in a way that produces peace (1 Tim 2:2). Draw them to repentance (Jn 16:8).

Bring godly, wise counselors alongside them in order to sustain our nation and produce peace and safety (Prv 11:14). Prompt within them a consideration of being held accountable for their decisions. Give courage, wisdom, and knowledge to make right decisions, and grant favor with others as they do (Ps 75:7; 2 Chr 19:5-7).

Remind us to pray for (1 Tim 2:1) and submit to the leaders you have placed over us as an act of submission to you (1 Pet 2:13-14). Help us rest in the fact that you control the heart of leaders like a stream of water in your hand (Prv 21:1) and that you are in fact the King of all the earth (Ps 47:7-9).

5.3.5. Judges and law enforcement.

God and Judge of all, make those who rule over us, rule with justice and a fear of you (2 Sm 23:3), for they do not judge for man but for you (2 Chro 19:6).

May we choose capable people, who fear you, love truth, and hate bribes (Ex 18:21); so justice may roll down like waters and righteousness flow like an ever-flowing stream (Amos 5:24).

Enable our leaders to defend the poor and fatherless, do justice to the afflicted and needy, rescuing the poor and needy from the wicked (Ps 82:3-4). May they never produce terror in those who do right, but rather in those doing wrong (Rom 13:3; 1 Pe 2:14).

5.4. Intercession for specific people groups.

5.4.1. Ministers of the Gospel.

Our Great Shepherd, teach our ministers how they ought to act among your people – the church of the living God, the pillar and foundation of the truth (1 Tim 3:15). May they do their best to present themselves to you as an approved workman, who doesn't need to be ashamed, correctly teaching your word (2 Tim 2:15).

Please protect them, both spiritually and physically, from Satan, the world, and their own sinful hearts (2 Pe 5:8; 2 Thes 3:2; Jn 17:15; Jas 1:14-15). Bring refreshment, primarily in Christ and His Word, but also from others (Rom 1:11-12; Ps 23:1-3; Ps 119:18).

May they be faithful, both in doctrine and in character (Rom 12:1-2; 1 Tim 4:16; 2 Tim 1:14). Grant them wisdom in ministry and in their lives (Jas 1:5; Prv 4:6-7). Strengthen their families, providing healthy marriages and well-maintained homes (Is 54:13; 1 Tim 3:2-6).

Enable them to give proper attention to reading, exhortation, and teaching, so they may save both themselves and their hearers (1 Tim 4:13-16). Make them competent in the Scriptures (Act 18:24), so their preaching is bold, powerful, effective, and clear (Eph 6:18-20; Tit 1:9; Col 4:2-4; Phil 1:18-20). May their leadership be characterized by humility, faithfulness, energy, and creativity (Josh 13:1; Matt 20:28; Phil 2:3).

Lord, grant that their labor is not in vain or their energy expended for nothing (Is 49:4), rather may your hand be with them and may many be turned to you through their ministry (Act 11:21).

5.4.2. A spouse.

Give them a desire for you beyond and above anything on earth. Help them find ultimate satisfaction in You (Ps 73:25). Like Moses, make them willing and desirous to go anywhere if and only if You are there (Ex 33:14–15). Increase their faith and produce ever increasing confidence that You are only working good for them (Rom 8:28). Help them see in Christ the beautiful radiance and imprint of Your character. Rescue them from despair by understanding Christ upholds the universe by his power (Heb 1:3). Allow an ever-increasing knowledge of Christ to bear fruit in the lives of others (Col 1:9). Through an increasing knowledge of Christ, deliver them from the defilements of the world (2 Pe 1:3, 2:20; Eph 3:19). Produce in them a desire to more and more cling to Christ and die to sin (Rom 6:11). Increase her desire to enhance her character (1 Pe 3:4). Help him love her as Christ loved the church, live with her in an understanding way, and show her honor (Eph 5:25–31).

5.4.3. The young.

Draw them to yourself through the convicting work of the Holy Spirit (Jn 16:8). Give them a good disposition and a healthy and stable mind, growing in wisdom and knowledge (Lk 2:52; Prv 5:1–2; Ps 111:10). Give them good health and preserve them from severely harmful accidents (3 Jn 2). Pour out Your Spirit upon them so they may serve You well in their generation (Jl 2:28–29; cf. Acts 2:14 ff). Let them find their greatest delight in walking in close fellowship with You (1 Jn 1:3–4). Fill them with Your Spirit, producing fruit and impacting those around them for Your glory (Eph 5:15–18). Keep them from the snare of evil company. Protect them amid temptation. Help them flee youthful lusts (1 Cor 15:33; 2 Tim 2:22). Let Christ be formed in their souls, so they love You with all their soul, heart, and mind (Matt 22:37–38).

5.4.4. Parents.

Help parents to know your love, believe in Jesus, and come to the light so they will not perish and have eternal life (Jn 3:16–21). Humble them. Have compassion on them. Satisfy their souls. Show your deeds. Establish their works (Ps 90:12–17). Speak through your word and give them wisdom and understanding. Protect and lead them (Prv 2:1–10). Bless their relationships with spouse, children, grandkids, friends, and church. Draw their hearts to you and in so doing produce within them hope, a glad heart, security, true life, and eternal pleasures (Ps 16:8–11). When anxiety creeps in, bring them peace by helping them rejoice in you, sense your presence, call out to you, and cling to Christ (Phil 4:4–9). Give parents an eternal perspective, accompanied by gratitude and trust in God's provisions and an ongoing pursuit of righteousness and avoidance of sin (1 Tim 6:6-12).

5.4.5. The old.

Our everlasting God, who does not faint or grow weary, we most certainly do grow weary and grow old. There are many who are old disciples of Jesus. May they continue to be fruitful for Christ (Ps 92:12–14). May they be encouraged and comforted by family and loved ones. May they not be lonely or disheartened (1 Thes 5:14; 2 Cor 7:13). Meet their daily needs of provisions, grace, peace, wisdom and strength (Ps 37:25). Help them use time wisely. May they encourage others and pray faithfully (Eph 5:16). Strengthen them to be found faithful to the end (2 Tim 4:7).

For those whom you have taught from their youth and who continue to proclaim your wondrous deeds, even when they are old and gray, do not forsake them. Do not cast them off in their old age. May they proclaim your glory to the next generation (Ps 71:17-18, 9).

5.4.6. The rich and prosperous.

Lord, keep those rich in this world not to be proud and not to trust in their money, which is so unreliable. Their trust should be in you who richly gives all we need for our enjoyment. Stir in them a desire to do good and be rich in good deeds, generous, and sharing with others. In so doing, encourage them and remind them they are storing up treasure as a good, future foundation so they may experience true life (1 Tim 6:17-19). Even though it is hard for a rich person to enter the kingdom of heaven, thankfully with you all things are possible (Matt 19:23, 26).

5.4.7. The poor and afflicted.

God, our great provider, you have chosen those who are poor in the world to be rich in faith and heirs of the kingdom (Ja 2:5) and recipients of the good news preached to them (Matt 11:5). You have promised to deliver the needy when they call for they have no one to defend them, and you've promised to show pity on the weak and save the lives of the needy. From oppression and violence, redeem them, for they are precious in your sight (Ps 72:14).

Even though the righteous person faces many troubles, you come to the rescue each time (Ps 34:19); and though affliction for the present seems grievous rather than joyous, you produce the peaceable fruit of righteousness in those who are trained by it (Heb 12:11).

5.4.8. The sick and suffering.

Father of compassion and God of all comfort, grant those who are sick to not despise your work, rather look to you as the author of life and death (Jb 5:6; Ps 68:20). If it be your will, give them good health (3 Jn 2). Comfort them (2 Cor 1:4). Secure their trust in you and steer them from self-reliance (Prv 3:5). Help them suffer well and commit themselves to your loving care (1 Pe 4:19). Grant them endurance and encouragement (Rom 15:4–6). Cause them to look to Jesus and not grow weary or lose heart (Heb 12:1–3). Give them peace in Christ (Is 26:3). Give them joy and keep them faithful amid tribulation (Rom 12:12). Allow them to be content in whatever circumstances you choose (Phil 4:11–13).

5.4.9. Our enemies and those that hate us.

Lord and Savior of those hostile to yourself, assist us in loving our enemies. May we pray for those who persecute us and treat us unjustly (Matt 5:44). Empower us to forgive them as Christ has forgiven us and may we have a spirit toward them as Stephen when he pleaded, "do not hold this sin against them" (Lk 23:34; Ac 7:60). Work in us the patience that bears with others and forgives them (Col 3:13). May our lives please you in such a way as to even bring peace to our enemies (Prv 16:7).

5.4.10. Our friends and those that love us.

Our Great God, and friend of sinners. We lift up to you our dear friends and those we love. Open their eyes even wider to You (Eph 1:15–18). Fully satisfy them with yourself (Ps 119:10, 15, 37, 133). Fill their hearts with love for others (Phil 1:9–11). Fill them with the knowledge and wisdom of Your will (Col 1:9–10). Give faith to trust through pain and disappointment (2 Cor 12:7-10). Give them boldness to speak about Jesus (Col 4:2–4; cf. Eph 6:19-20). Send them wise and godly friends (1 Thes 3:9–10; cf. Rom 1:9–10; 15:30-33). Protect them from enemies of their soul (2 Thes 3:1–2) and from making other areas of life a god (Col 3:23-24). Keep them from conforming to the world and instead conform them to the image of Christ (Phil 1:9-11). Magnify Jesus' value to others through their lives (2 Thes 1:11–12). Thank You for the evidence of working in their lives (Rom 1:8; 1 Cor 1:4–7; Eph 1:15–16; Phil 1:3–5; 1 Thes 1:2–3; 2 2 Thes 1:3).

And we wish for all those whom we love in the truth, that they may prosper in every way and be in good health physically just as they are spiritually (1 Jn 1-2). May the grace of the Lord Jesus Christ be with their spirits (Phlm 25).

6.
THINGS TO PRAY
FOR PEOPLE

6.1. Praying for Those You Love.

(1) Open their eyes even wider to You (Eph 1:15–18). (2) Fully satisfy them with yourself (Ps 119:10, 15, 37, 133). (3) Fill their hearts with love for others (Phil 1:9–11). (4) Fill them with the knowledge and wisdom of Your will (Col 1:9–10). (5) Give faith to trust through pain and disappointment (2 Cor 12:7-10). (6) Give them boldness to speak about Jesus (Col 4:2–4; cf. Eph 6:19-20). (7) Send them wise and godly friends (1 Thes 3:9–10; cf. Rom 1:9–10; 15:30-33). (8) Protect them from enemies of their soul (2 Thes 3:1–2) and from making other areas of life a god (Col 3:23-24). (9) Keep them from conforming to the world and instead conform them to the image of Christ (Phil 1:9-11). (10) Magnify Jesus' value to others through their lives (2 Thes 1:11–12). (11) Thank You for the evidence of working in their lives (Rom 1:8; 1 Cor 1:4–7; Eph 1:15–16; Phil 1:3–5; 1 Thes 1:2–3; 2 2 Thes 1:3).

May they
Open their eyes wider to you and your Word,
Trust through pain and disappointment, and have
Hearts filled with a knowledge of you and a love for others.
Equip them with boldness to declare Jesus and fight the enemies of their soul.
Bring them
Relationships that are both wise and godly, yet ultimately
Satisfy them with yourself.

6.2. Praying For a Spouse.

(1) Give them a desire for you beyond and above anything on earth. Help them find ultimate satisfaction in You (Ps 73:25). (2) Like Moses, make them willing and desirous to go anywhere if and only if You are there (Ex 33:14–15). (3) Increase their faith and produce ever increasing confidence that You are only working good for them (Rom 8:28). (4) Help them see in Christ the beautiful radiance and imprint of Your character. Rescue them from despair by understanding Christ upholds the universe by his power (Heb 1:3). (5) Allow an ever-increasing knowledge of Christ to bear fruit in the lives of others (Col 1:9). (6) Through an increasing knowledge of Christ, deliver them from the defilements of the world (2 Pe 1:3, 2:20; Eph 3:19). (7) Produce in them a desire to more and more cling to Christ and die to sin (Rom 6:11). (8) Increase her desire to enhance her character (1 Pe 3:4). (9) Help him love her as Christ loved the church, live with her in an understanding way, and show her honor (Eph 5:25–31).

Make her willing & desirous to go anywhere if & only if you are there.
Allow an ever increasing knowledge of Christ to:
Rescue her from despair &
Rescue her from the defilements of the world & her own sinful heart.
Increase her faith & desire to cling to Christ.
Allow her to see in Christ the radiance of your character,
Giving her a desire for & ultimate satisfaction in you.
Enhance her pursuit of godly character,
        & his pursuit of loving like Christ and showing honor.

6.3. Praying for Your Children.

(1) Draw them to yourself through the convicting work of the Holy Spirit (Jn 16:8). (2) Give them a good disposition and a healthy and stable mind, growing in wisdom and knowledge (Lk 2:52; Prv 5:1–2; Ps 111:10). (3) Give them good health and preserve them from

severely harmful accidents (3 Jn 2). (4) Pour out Your Spirit upon them so they may serve You well in their generation (Jl 2:28–29; cf. Acts 2:14 ff). (5) Let them find their greatest delight in walking in close fellowship with You (1 Jn 1:3–4). (6) Fill them with Your Spirit, producing fruit and impacting those around them for Your glory (Eph 5:15–18). (7) Keep them from the snare of evil company. Protect them amid temptation. Help them flee youthful lusts (1 Cor 15:33; 2 Tim 2:22). (8) Let Christ be formed in their souls, so they love You with all their soul, heart, and mind (Matt 22:37–38).

Grant that
Christ is formed in their souls & the
Holy Spirit fills them, producing joyful service & eternal fruit.
Increase their knowledge and wisdom.
Look after their physical needs, protecting & providing what is sufficient.

Empower them to
Delight in walking with you & in your Word &
Resists youthful lusts & evil company.

Assist us in
Entrusting them to your care,
Needing your wisdom & grace to guide them & model a godly example.

6.4. Praying for Your Church.

(1) Produce unity amid diversity (Rom 12:5; cf. Jesus prayer for unity in Jn 17:20-23; Paul's exhortation to the church to pursue unity in Eph 4:3; and a future picture of this unity in heaven in Rv 7:9). (2) Form a church community that expects and exhibits discipleship as an ordinary part of the Christian life (2 Tim 2:2; cf. the Great Commission in Matt 28:19-20, and a model by Paul of life-on-life discipleship in 1 Thes 2:8). (3) Prepare faithful elders to use Scripture to equip members to do the work of ministry, resulting in the

discipleship of all ages throughout the church (2 Tim 4:2; Eph 4:12; 2 Tim 2:2). (4) Give our church a hunger for scriptural truth (2 Tim 3:14–16). (5) Produce in us meaningful transparent relationships. Allow isolation and anonymity to become abnormal (Acts 2:44–45; Eph 4:15–16). (6) Produce preaching that is both Biblical and Spirit empowered (Acts 6:4; Heb 3:7). (7) Keep our elders and leadership above reproach and fit for ministry (1 Tim 3:1; Titus 1:6). (8) Help us grow in prayer (Phil 4:6; Lk 18:1; Jer 33:3). (9) Empower us and give us a desire to be distinct from the world (Rom 12:1–2; cf. Eph 4:17, 1 Jn 2:15-17). (10) Embolden us to share the gospel and see more conversions. Prompt more members to consider their careers as an avenue to take the gospel to new places (Acts 1:8; cf. Matt 28:19-20). (11) Prepare us for persecution (2 Tim 3:12). (12) Help us find hope in heaven and not in earthly politics (Rom 13:1; 2 Pe 3:13). (13) Help us give with joy as we give faithfully and sacrificially (2 Cor 9:7).

Produce
Biblical, Spirit-empowered preaching,
Oneness in Christ & truth amid diversity,
Discipleship that is ordinary, expected, & intergenerational,
Yearning for meaningful, transparent relationships.
Prepare your church for
Oppression by spiritual forces and persecution by the world,
Faithful elders to use scripture to equip others for the work of ministry.
Preserve the
Character of leadership as above reproach & fit for ministry,
Hunger for scriptural truth,
Rigorous pursuit & desire for holiness,
Inspired by our hope in heaven & not earthly politics;
Sacrificial, faithful, & joyful giving and service; and a
Tireless proclamation of the Gospel.

6.5. Praying for Pastors.

(1) Protection, both spiritual and physical, from Satan, the world, and their own sinful heart (2 Pe 5:8; 2 Thes 3:2; Jn 17:15; Jas 1:14-15). (2) Refreshment, primarily in Christ and His Word, but also from others (Rom 1:11-12; Ps 23:1-3; Ps 119:18). (3) Faithfulness, both in doctrine and character (Rom 12:1-2; 1 Tim 4:16; 2 Tim 1:14). (4) Wisdom (Jas 1:5; Prv 4:6-7). (5) Family, healthy marriage and well maintained home (Is 54:13; 1 Tim 3:2-6). (6) Preaching that is bold, powerful, effective, and clear (Eph 6:18-20; Tit 1:9; Col 4:2-4; Phil 1:18-20). (7) Leadership that is humble, faithful, energetic, and creative (Josh 13:1; Matt 20:28; Phil 2:3).

Powerful, bold, effective, and clear preaching

An abiding, healthy marriage and well maintained home

Strong, humble, faithful, and creative leadership

Teaching and character that are faithful

Oversight of church that is wise, patient, and courageous

Refreshment in Christ and His Word, and from others

Spiritual and physical protection from Satan, the world, and their own sinful hearts.

6.6. Praying for Retirees and Parents.

[Retirees] (1) May they continue to be fruitful for Christ (Ps 92:12–14). (2) May they be encouraged and comforted by family and loved ones. May they not be lonely or disheartened (1 Thes 5:14; 2 Cor 7:13). (3) Meet their daily needs of provisions, grace, peace, wisdom and strength (Ps 37:25). (4) Help them use time wisely. May they encourage others and pray faithfully (Eph 5:16). (5) Strengthen them to be found faithful to the end (2 Tim 4:7). [Parents] (1) Help my parents to know your love, believe in Jesus, and come to the light so they will not perish and have eternal life (Jn 3:16–21). (2) Humble them. Have compassion on them. Satisfy their souls. Show your deeds. Establish their works (Ps 90:12–17). (3) Speak through your word and give them wisdom and understanding. Protect and lead them (Prv 2:1–10). (4) Bless their relationships with spouse, children, grandkids, friends, and church. (5) Draw their hearts to you and in so doing produce within them hope, a glad heart, security, true life, and eternal pleasures (Ps 16:8–11). (6) When anxiety creeps in, bring them peace by helping them rejoice in you, sense your presence, call out to you, and cling to Christ (Phil 4:4–9). (7) Give my parents an eternal perspective, accompanied by gratitude and trust in God's provisions and an ongoing pursuit of righteousness and avoidance of sin (1 Tim 6:6-12).

Redeem their time with wisdom, encouraging others and faithfully praying.
Encourage and comfort them with your presence amid anxiety.
Take care of their daily needs of provision, grace, peace, and strength.
Incline their hearts to you, producing hope, security, and life.
    Grant
Relationships so as not to be lonely or disheartened, an
Eternal perspective, accompanied by gratitude and trust, and an
Enduring pursuit of righteousness and avoidance of sin.
Strengthen them to be found faithful and fruitful for Christ, until the end.

6.7. Praying for the Persecuted Church.

(1) Send them relief from heaven above. Deliver your saints from hateful enemies too strong for them (Heb 13:3; Ps 18:16–19). (2) Preserve the righteous from being tempted to respond in sinful ways to their mistreatment (Lk 6:27–31). (3) Strengthen the patience and faith of your suffering saints (Rv 13:10; Lam 3:26). (4) Give them boldness to speak your truth with the right words in the right timing (Eph 6:19–20). (5) Grace them with an understanding and experience of your peace amid their weakness. Give them hope (2 Cor 12:9). (6) Draw them to you for their power (2 Cor 1:7–9). (7) Be present and protect them according to your will (Matt 26:39). (8) Hear their prayers (Ps 79:11). (9) Open the eyes and soften the hearts of those who are persecuting (Matt 5:44; Eze 18:23).

Preserve the righteous from sinful responses to their mistreatment.
Equip them with boldness to speak your truth accurately and timely.
Regard their prayers and send heavenly relief.
Strengthen the patience and faith of your suffering servants.
Encourage them through the presence of other believers, while ultimately
Clinging to you for their power.
    Assist them in
Understanding and experiencing your peace amid their weakness.
Transform the hearts and open the eyes of those who are persecuting them.
Embrace them with the hope and peace of your presence.
Deliver your saints from hateful enemies.

6.8. Praying for the Sick & Suffering.

(1) Grant those who are sick to not despise your work, rather look to you as the author of life and death (Jb 5:6; Ps 68:20). (2) If it be your will, give them good health (3 Jn 2; potentially Jas 5:14). (3) Comfort them (2 Cor 1:4). (4) Secure their trust in you and steer them from self-reliance (Prv 3:5). (5) Help them suffer well and commit

themselves to your loving care (1 Pe 4:19). (6) Grant them endurance and encouragement (Rom 15:4–6). (7) Cause them to look to Jesus and not grow weary or lose heart (Heb 12:1–3). (8) Give them peace in Christ (Is 26:3). (9) Give them joy and keep them faithful amid tribulation (Rom 12:12). (10) Allow them to be content in whatever circumstances you choose (Phil 4:11–13).

Secure their trust in you and steer them from self-reliance.
Inspire them to look to Jesus and not grow weary or lose heart.
Comfort them and grant them endurance.
Keep them content, committing themselves to your loving care, in whatever circumstances you choose.

6.9. Praying for the Lost.

(1) Send your Spirit to convict and draw unbelievers to yourself (Jn 16:8; Eze 36:27). (2) Remove their heart of stone and give them a new heart (Eze 11:19). (3) Open their eyes to see the truth so that they will repent and call on the name of the Lord and be saved (Acts 3:19; Rom 10:13; 2 Tim 2:25–26). (4) Bring believers into their lives who will live out and verbally share the gospel with them. Help me to be sensitive to whom you would have me share the gospel with and then the boldness and grace to do so (Rom 10:14).

Lead believers (if not me) into their lives who will live out and verbally share the gospel.
Open their eyes to see the truth, leading to repentance and salvation.
Send your Spirit to convict and draw unbelievers to yourself.
Transform their hearts of stone by giving them a new heart.

6.10. Praying for Political Leaders.

May they lead in a way that produces peace (1 Tim 2:2). Draw them to repentance (Jn 16:8). Bring godly, wise counselors alongside them (Prv 11:14). Prompt within them a consideration of being held accountable for their decisions. Give courage, wisdom, and knowledge to make right decisions, and grant favor with others as they do (Ps 75:7; 2 Chr 19:5-7). Remind us to pray for (1Tim 2:1) and submit to the leaders you have placed over us as an act of submission to you (1 Pet 2:13-14). Help us rest in the fact that you control the heart of leaders like a stream of water in your hand (Prv 21:1) and that you are in fact the King of all the earth (Ps 47:7-9).

May their leadership
Produce peace.
Open their hearts and minds to wise counselors.
Limit their impact when self-serving, yet
Ingratiate them to others when leading well.
Train them to weigh the divine accountability for their decisions.
Increase wisdom, courage, and knowledge.
May we
Calm our hearts, knowing you are the King, holding the heart of every leader and
Submit to our leaders as an act of submission to you not merely out of respect for them.